PRAISE FOR *COMPA*

Mary Joy and I believe in the global impact that MedSend has had. Reading this book and its individual stories has opened our eyes to the sacrifices made and blessings received in order to deliver the love of God through healthcare in low-resource areas of the world. This is the love of Jesus exhibited in tangible ways—a roadmap for the next generation. It is exciting to be a part of this wonderful journey of love!

—JERRE AND MARY JOY STEAD,
CEO of 21 public companies (Jerre), Visionaries and Philanthropists, Founders of Stead Impact Ventures and Foundation

Here, presented in captivating narratives, is a display of the power of God in life stories of ordinary people doing extraordinary exploits. Medical missions have always opened frontiers to missions. Modern-day frontiers present extraordinary opportunities for God to pen stories of His people, of whom He is not ashamed. In spite of pain, heartaches, loss, and attacks by the evil one, for these it will be said: *They triumphed over him by the blood of the Lamb and by the word of their testimony; they did not love their lives so much as to shrink from death.* Revelation 12:11

—DR. FLORENCE MUINDI,
Founder and President of Life In Abundance International

God is on the move in mission hospitals around the world. You won't see it in the news, and you might not even hear about it at your local church. But I see it happening every day through the talented healthcare missionaries who leave lucrative careers to serve in places you may not be able to find on a map. Their stories are a blessing to us all. In *Compassionate Love*, Rick draws our attention to some extraordinary Jesus-following doctors who pour out their lives for their patients, their God, and the next generation of healthcare workers in the nations where they serve. This book is a beautiful reminder that God uses His people to bring healing and good news to a hurting world.

—JUSTIN NARDUCCI,
President and CEO of CURE International Children's Hospitals

As followers of Christ, God calls upon us all to go and serve—some locally, some to the foreign mission field. *Compassionate Love* is a soul-searching and compelling introspection of our own life journey and where God just might be calling us next.

—DR. LANCE PLYLER,
Chief Medical Officer at Samaritan's Purse

Missionary martyr Jim Elliot famously said, "He is no fool who gives what he cannot keep to gain what he cannot lose." In this wonderful volume, Rick Allen shares the stories of some of this world's least foolish people. Refusing to be seduced by the enticements of worldly success, they dare to believe that the way of cruciform love marked out by Jesus is truly the path to a life of abundance and significance. Missionaries are my favorite people, and some of my most favorite people are included in this book. Thank God for MedSend who helps make these stories possible, and thank God for Rick Allen, who has shared these stories with you and me.

—STAN KEY,
Minister at Large, OneWay Ministries

At first glance, *Compassionate Love* by Rick Allen might seem like a book about medicine and medical missions. On the contrary, it is a book about much more. It is the story of a compassionate God making an impact on the lives of people who are destitute, neglected, and discarded in some of the hardest places in the world. It is the story of ordinary men and women who have surrendered their lives to be used by God to make an extraordinary impact through love, compassion, and the gospel. It is also the story of an organization that God has placed at the juncture of these incredible human needs and the men and women who are God's hands and feet for meeting those needs. This is a book for students of missions and for veteran missionaries. It is for donors and for those who are called to go. It is for pastors and for those in the pew. I highly recommend it.

—JOSHUA BOGUNJOKO,
Former International Director of SIM

In this amazing book, Rick Allen tells stories that need to be told of ordinary people who, by the grace of God and with love for others, do extraordinary things. These intimate vignettes also show that small organizations supported by individual donors can be catalysts for meeting spiritual and healthcare needs across the globe. What a blessing it is to catch a glimpse of God working to heal hurting people.

—DOUGLAS A. DREVETS, MD, DTM&H, FIDSA,
Regents' Professor and Chief of Infectious Diseases at University of
Oklahoma Health Sciences Center; Chair of MedSend Board of Directors

I first met Rick Allen at a Medical Missions Summit sponsored by MedSend and CMDA. As we shared stories about medical missionaries and the extreme suffering that some of them face, his pastor's heart was immediately obvious. The stories he tells in this book highlight his considerable abilities and energy in the support of and care for those committed to serving the Lord in medical missions. As is so well illustrated in this book, the result has been the advancement of the kingdom and enriching the lives of those committed to the kingdom. I urge anyone considering a call to serve in healthcare to digest and reflect on the challenges Rick offers.

—JARRETT RICHARDSON, MD

You may have a hard time putting this book down! The suspenseful stories of healthcare missionaries that Rick Allen so compellingly shares showcase what our compassionate and loving God does when normal people follow the challenging calling to love others on His behalf. You will find yourself transported into the inner world of those following this call—the excitement of seeing God at work as well as the anguish of facing so many deaths and encountering spiritual questions in the crucible of so much human suffering. Both those who wonder about their own calling and those who support the healthcare mission movement will find inspiration in this book.

—**FRAUKE C. SCHAEFER, MD**

There are a few books that have left me with a deep-felt longing to continue absorbing what I've just experienced and what it means for my life. *Compassionate Love* has been one of those for me. The intimate stories of these healthcare workers, the sacrificial decisions they have been called to make, God's comforting presence in disturbing situations, and the tangible way God has used them to heal both the bodies and the souls of those who suffer, draw me to listen for God's invitation to walk even closer by His side. As a counselor, I've had the opportunity to walk with those in the global healthcare ministry. The stories in this book capture just a glimpse of what God is doing to reach people across the world and in some of the most difficult situations. God's love is steadfast, creative, and continually amazing!

—**CHARLIE SCHAEFER, PH.D.,**
Barnabas International

COMPASSIONATE
LOVE

Blessings Rich

How God is Blessing a Hurting World

RICK ALLEN

Published by Storybuilders Press
Hardcover: 978-1-954521-26-1
Paperback: 978-1-954521-27-8
eBook: 978-1-954521-28-5
Audio: 978-1-954521-29-2

This book and my life are dedicated to my wife, Linda, our four amazing daughters, Kirsten, Carly, Dana, and Tracy, and the three well-above-average grandchildren they have blessed us with. I love you more!

TABLE OF CONTENTS

PREFACE

This is a book of extraordinary stories from around the world. It's a book about ordinary people . . . and the extraordinary God they serve.

You'll read of men and women in the field of healthcare who have responded to God's call and have found themselves in unlikely situations and circumstances, completely out of their comfort zone, in total dependence on Him.

But they wouldn't be living out such extraordinary stories without the support of other ordinary people. The ministry of MedSend is made up of people with varied backgrounds: business people, career military personnel, counselors, marketing professionals, writers, insurance salespeople, and nurses. They are ordinary people responding to God and His calling. MedSend donors support from home so others can go.

God calls all of us in one way or another. Some serve God and His church around the block from where they live and others in faraway places. As you read this book, I pray you will find a path forward toward *your* call.

God has designed an exciting place for you to live out His call on your life. Peace, joy, and contentment come from following Him.

It is an incredible journey.

Rick Allen

CHAPTER 1

THE BROKEN WORLD

P lease consider asking a group of friends or associates the following question:

As you observe the world around us, do you see things getting better or worse?

What kind of responses do you think you would get? My guess is that most people, without even thinking twice, would respond that it's getting worse. Much worse. There are lots of reasons for this. It may be that they watch the news, and it's all doom and gloom. It may be that their social media is an echo chamber of "us" versus "them." It may be that they are right.

After all, as I write this book, Israel is again at war, Russia has invaded an independent nation, new variants of COVID are being discovered, inflation is skyrocketing, suicide and drug addiction are rampant, and the list goes on.

Oh yeah, and China and the United States are taunting one another, and the global economy is teetering toward meltdown!

It's easy to see all that and wonder what in the world is going on. More specifically, where in the world is God?

People have been asking that question for as long as there have been, well, people.

Life is messy. Poverty, natural disasters, famine, wars, and violence are abundant. All it takes is a quick look at the news to see that the world is not as it should be. If you're a Christ follower, you can trace this problem back to a garden.

Even if you are living in relative comfort and safety, largely un-affected by global disasters, on a personal level, troubles are never far away. Illness, broken relationships, financial woes, stressful work, a lack of purpose . . . life can feel hard, hopeless even.

It raises more questions. Real questions. Raw questions.

In the midst of despair, where do we find hope?

In the midst of loneliness, where do we find community?

Does God care about what's going on in the world? Does God care about you and me?

The short answer is yes. God does care. And I know it because of two things. First, because He sent Jesus. In Jesus, we see God's response to pain on earth. By sending Jesus to earth, God joined us in our suffering. Jesus spent his earthly life among suffering and marginalized people. He responded to hurting people with sadness and grief.

He wept. He touched them, offering both physical and spiritual healing.

And then, remarkably, he asked his followers to do the same. I see God's care in the world and in my own life through the care of other Christians. The world is wracked with pain and suffering, but there is also a lot of good being done in the world. It may not be getting a lot of press, but there are countless Christians who are messengers of hope in a hurting world.

Hope promises that someday all will be made right, but until then, God evidently prefers not to intervene in every instance of evil or heartache, no matter how devastating. Rather, He's asked His followers to do it.

In the midst of a hostile, sad, lonely world, He's asked us to share His love.

Best of all, He's equipped us to do that in a way that is unique and different for each person. What does it look like? It can play out in many different ways. For followers of Jesus, the path of following God's call on our lives is not always smooth or straight. But it almost always starts with surrender. That has certainly been true in my life.

A LIFE OF SURRENDER

In the summer of 2001, I found myself unemployed from my dream job at the pinnacle of my successful twenty-five-year career. Due to the economic downturn and the dot-com bust, for the first time since high school, I wasn't working. For the most part, I accepted it as a chance to rest. I took advantage of summer vacation to enjoy being with my wife and four daughters. I took my mother to Ireland to visit her ancestral home. I figured I'd simply find another job in the fall when the kids went back to school.

September came, and with it, the 9/11 terrorist attacks. I was living in Connecticut at the time and had been commuting to New York City for years. That tragedy changed everything. Not only could I not find a job, but for the first time, I came face-to-face with the fact that I was not in control. Maybe that should have been obvious to me long before then—I'm sure there had been moments—but I'd never experienced such a complete upending as I did that fall.

Talk about the world not being as it should be. Not only was the nation in shock and turmoil, but so was I. How could this happen in America? Why would God allow this kind of devastation? My personal sense of upheaval was overwhelming. Full of questions and uncertainty about the path forward, this combination of national and personal events kick-started a season of intentional surrender in my life.

In the next few years, the Lord asked me to surrender. Surrender the high-tech career, the house on the beach, the fast cars and other toys I'd accumulated, the Christian education for my children, all the elements of the plan I had made for myself. All I asked was that God not take my family.

Eight years later, everything I had thought was important was reduced to nothing. Yet my family had transitioned through this life change intact.

For someone who was used to being in control, it was jarring. I was adrift. Fortunately, that's often where God can do His best work in us.

Through a series of providential events, I wound up both pastoring a church and running a medical missions organization. As you can imagine, that was a big shift from the tech world.

How did I get there?

The short version of the long story is that not being able to find a job, I started an independent consulting business to help Christian business owners actively apply their faith in their businesses and careers. Because of my extensive business background, I also helped multiple people start or turn around businesses.

In addition, while serving as an elder at Black Rock Church, my fellow elders asked me if I would pastor a small church in

Stamford, Connecticut, which had experienced a split. The intent was to turn it around and help it grow.

I had become "the turnaround guy."

Through a family acquaintance, my daughter picked up a two-week job filing papers in the office of a nonprofit organization called MedSend while home from college. One day her car needed an oil change, so my wife dropped her off and stayed to chat a bit with the office manager, who explained that MedSend was experiencing some challenges.

My wife came home and asked, "Have you ever considered helping MedSend? It sounds like they could use someone like you."

That's how I came to MedSend. All because of an oil change.

I went into the challenge excited.

Thirty days later, I was thinking, *Lord, what in the world am I doing here?*

Then the financial crisis of 2008 hit, and I started to realize why I was at MedSend. This was going to be a turnaround, and it was going to be challenging.

My office was a converted storage closet. Throughout the day, I crunched numbers and arranged meetings, all the while surrendering my plans and ideas to the Lord. It soon became clear that the challenges facing MedSend were beyond my skills. I could not turn this organization around. God would have to show up.

As God was building my faith, He was also challenging much of what I thought I knew about missions and Christ's followers making a difference in the world.

To me, like to many in my generation, missions mostly meant evangelism. It meant Westerners (usually Americans) raising financial support and traveling across the ocean to evangelize, convert, and baptize believers and then plant churches. It meant regular progress reports and prayer cards posted on the refrigerator.

Then I met Tom and Libby Little, and it changed the way I viewed mission work. And missionaries. And myself. The Littles were MedSend grant recipients working in Afghanistan, and through their sacrifice, my eyes were opened to how God uses ordinary people in extraordinary ways to share His love.

You'll learn their whole story later, but when we first crossed paths, Tom and Libby were in the United States to attend a conference in Boston. As they passed by the MedSend office, we met for lunch, and for the next three hours, I listened to them explain what their life on the other side of the world was like.

They had been in Afghanistan since the 1970s, through all kinds of political and personal upheaval: the revolution, the Soviet invasion, the takeover by the Taliban, and the American invasion.

I was enthralled.

Here was a couple living out the call of God by providing much-needed medical care and spiritual encouragement in dire, dangerous circumstances.

Here was a couple actively doing something to offer hope and healing in Jesus's name. This was a true expression of living out a Christian mission.

I was hooked. God had me exactly where I needed to be.

WHY MEDICAL MISSIONS?

Tom and Libby Little were well acquainted with the fact that all was not as it should be. Their daily lives were wracked with war, violence, poverty, and upheaval all around. But they dedicated their lives to serving God by serving others. As a medical professional, Tom was able to share the love of Christ simply by *doing what he'd been trained to do.*

Today, more than ever before, due to political and cultural changes in many countries, healthcare gives believers access to places where other forms of Christian witness do not work. Mission-sending organizations report that over *half* the world's nations will not issue a missionary visa. But a healthcare visa? That's among the top four professional visas being issued. The world is changing, and this presents a special opportunity to send Christ-following healthcare workers to even the most difficult places.

On a global scale, the need for medical care is dire. According to the World Health Organization, the world needs seven million more healthcare professionals to meet a minimum standard of patient care worldwide. This means that trained medical professionals are welcome in almost any country in the world outside of the West. Medicine is one of the few professions that gives missionaries an open door to the unreachable.

The harvest is plentiful.

And the next generation is rising to meet the challenge. Perhaps more than any other generation, Gen Z is fueled by purpose. Having experienced a global pandemic, economic recessions, and major cultural shifts during formative periods in their lives, they see the world and their place in it differently. They want a chance to be part of something bigger than themselves.

Where older people like myself often drew a solid line between evangelism and humanitarian work, Christian young people today do not. To their way of thinking, the two must be intentionally intertwined. And as the first fully digital generation, for them, global connections are easier to make than ever.

It's no surprise that young professionals are emerging from their medical training with an increased interest in serving abroad. They want to be engaged globally, and they want to use their medical skills to do it. By creating cross-cultural relationships and providing compassionate care in Jesus's name, they have the opportunity to share him with a hurting world.

That's where MedSend comes in.

MedSend exists to help them get there, in spite of being saddled with significant educational debt. Since its founding in 1992, MedSend (as of this writing) has empowered more than 700 healthcare professionals to serve around the world in areas of deep physical and spiritual need by paying medical professionals' education loans while they serve long-term. MedSend grant recipients work at mission hospitals and rural clinics, train national healthcare professionals, and through involvement in community health education programs, help transform community and national healthcare systems.

Building on a sturdy foundation of missionary work in the last century, many of today's medical missionaries have their eyes set not only on compassionate care but also on multiplication. MedSend steps into this shift with the National Scholars Program, which sponsors advanced medical training for Christian national physicians in Africa and Asia. The goals of the program are simple but significant: (1) enable nationals to deliver high-quality healthcare in areas of high need—usually in their own countries; (2) empower nationals to become the trainers of future medical professionals; and (3) by working with the national governments, transform healthcare systems within their home countries.

Every day it is more difficult to get into countries with the message of the gospel. Yet at the same time, countries are becoming more desperate for medical personnel, and more Christian young people are heeding the call to go. It's not surprising—God always has a plan.

Jesus is the example. He *showed* people his Father; he *taught* the good news, and he *healed* people—all with a heart of compassion and an openness to go where the need was great.

Medical missionaries, in very practical ways, do what Jesus did.

Following the call to be a medical missionary is not easy, but a life of faith is not an easy one for anyone. It's not just missionaries. Whether at home or abroad, every believer at one time or another has to wrestle through what it means to fully follow Christ.

We all have to ask: *What does it mean to surrender everything and be used by God?*

ONLY ONE AGENDA

On the following pages, I will share the stories of normal, everyday people with one agenda: to be the hands and feet of Jesus Christ, bringing a compassionate love to the world. My prayer is that this book will show you God's love in action.

Not just that, though. I hope it will *challenge you* to take action in a way that aligns with your mission and calling. And at the end of the book, I'll show you how to discover what that looks like practically in your own life.

Many of the people you'll meet in these pages have given up everything to serve in unimaginable conditions. They've walked away from the prestige of being a healthcare provider in the United States and everything that often comes with that—the private practice, the big house, the country club. They are bringing a tangible expression of God's love, often in miraculous ways, often in harsh places.

Others you'll read about have overcome great odds to serve in their own countries. I want to honor their stories and inspire you to see God at work.

This book is not about me. It's not really even about MedSend. This book is about God and the amazing work He's doing through healthcare providers who have surrendered their lives to Him and to serving "the least of these" (Mt 25:45).

Ministering as a medical professional offers a unique opportunity to combine compassion and evangelism. Maybe you've never heard of medical missions. That's not surprising, given that medical-focused mission efforts only account for ten percent of missionary work around the globe. It's an untold story that needs to be told.

Whether it's through Western or national missionaries, I want your eyes to be opened to the new thing that God is doing around the world. And as you see example after example of how God is using people to make a difference, maybe you'll be inspired to think about your own life.

Because this book is also about you and where you fit in the story.

You have a role to play, a gift to give, a mission to pursue, and a calling to fulfill. When you do, you begin to see that in this uncertain world, God is still in control. He is still at work. And He is calling you to go, to love bigger, to serve better.

And through tiny steps of obedience, we can change the world.

CHAPTER 2

CATHY AND BUBBA HOELZER

DANGEROUS

A called person is dangerous to the enemy. And make no mistake, Bubba and Cathy Hoelzer are *called* people. God has used them to push back the darkness in some of the hardest and most difficult places on earth. God is in the business of changing individual hearts and lives, and it's through those individuals that God also changes nations.

When Bubba and Cathy got married, they knew God was calling them to go to places that others could not. Would not. Over several decades of serving God in these places, they have seen ample evidence of God's faithfulness.

From Turkey to Iraq to Sudan and Jordan, Bubba and Cathy are no strangers to difficulty. Their story begins with Cathy as a young missionary teaching English in Turkey. When the Gulf War began, Cathy found herself doing much more than teaching English pronunciation and subject-verb agreement. After volunteering in the Kurdish refugee camps, she moved to Kurdistan to direct a humanitarian program. Soon she was dodging bullets and working with refugees who were suffering from severe hunger and malnutrition. Despite having only been trained in primary healthcare at YWAM, God gave her insight into what a patient needed and a willingness to jump in wherever she could.

Though she had already experienced the challenges that come from being a young blond American woman in a Muslim country, they were nothing compared to the terror of an active war zone. Not only was she navigating cultural differences and expectations, but now she was also concerned for her life.

The first time she remembers really feeling afraid is when she was driving through the streets in Iraq with a supervisor and chaos broke loose around her.

As bullets flew around her, she screamed, "We have to get out of here! Turn around! Turn around!"

But as if a metaphor for the next several decades of her life, she and her driver went straight ahead—into the danger. Because sometimes the only way out is through.

GOD'S CALL–THE BACKSTORY

Cathy grew up in a dysfunctional, alcoholic home—not the ideal setting that you might imagine a missionary to come from. But God's plan prevails. Teenage years of drug addiction and a life that was far from God led to three years of intense searching before coming to Christ in a powerful way. As a new believer, she joined prayer groups for missions and began reading missionary letters. These accounts got her excited about the spread of the gospel around the world.

On a mission trip to Mexico, reading a book called *Operation World*, she learned that Turkey was the least evangelized nation in the world.

So what did Cathy do? She got her degree in teaching English and made her way to Turkey. From there, she eventually ended up in Iraq.

God has a plan even when we can't see it, and the gifts Cathy had for medicine were evident. She had no formal training. What she did have was an interest in nutrition gleaned from her mom, who was a dietitian. The medical needs due to hunger and malnutrition were staggering and not something local doctors had the means to effectively combat. Cathy jumped in, serving the best way she knew how and helping develop agricultural programs, including developing a nutrition source made from corn and soya blend. She even helped develop a hospital focused on treating malnutrition.

As she found herself caught up in simply serving people, God seemed to give her supernatural wisdom for their needs. She fell in love with medicine and thought, *What a great way to minister to people with the love of Christ.*

During this time she met a physician assistant (PA). This changed her life. She'd never heard of that pathway but was intrigued by the thought that she could practice medicine without the long-time commitment it took to become a doctor.

After three years in Iraq, she returned to the United States and actively set her heart on becoming a PA. Following that, she acquired her master's degree in public health.

Oh, and one more thing—a husband named Bubba.

TIP OF THE SPEAR FOR THE GOSPEL

Bubba Hoelzer, like Cathy, was convinced of the call of God on his life. Like the Apostle Paul, he wanted to serve in places where others did not. He didn't want to be bumping elbows with other missionaries. He wanted to go beyond . . . to the places where people are most ready to hear the gospel. When you look at him now—shaved head, bronzed by the sun—he looks like he's been carved from the rocky desert places he's called home for decades.

It's no wonder he's thrived there. He knew that in hard places where the pressure is intense and oppression is ongoing, people get to the point where they're no longer afraid to choose the things that they really want to choose.

That's where the gospel really can penetrate.

After marrying, Bubba and Cathy followed God's call together to war-torn Sudan. Equipped with her PA training, Cathy worked in a hospital. With grit and determination, Bubba rolled up his sleeves and got to work. He constructed clinics, staff homes, and other outbuildings. He installed solar panels and did everything he could to make the missionaries' lives more comfortable.

Together Cathy and Bubba worked in three different places in Sudan. There were no doctors, only Kenyan and American nurses and nurse practitioners, and only Kenyan clinical officers. Bubba supported these medical practitioners and their families in myriad ways and actively discipled and taught the people there. They formed a great team.

The need was great both in the hospital and in the outlying villages. And yet, their challenges seemed greater. In some of the remote villages, children would scream and run when they saw them coming. They'd never seen a white person before. Progress was slow. Sometimes it felt as if nothing was happening, as if they were treading through mud.

And yet, Bubba says it's in Sudan that he most clearly heard from God. In a place where he had no choice but to depend on God, walking by faith was an everyday, every-hour thing. And God kept asking them to stay, to keep going, to keep discipling, to keep teaching God's Word—especially to young men.

Now, years later, they see that God was working His plan. Amazingly, some of those frightened little children and gangly teenagers they referred to as their sons are now military intelligence and government leaders. Because of Bubba and Cathy's influence, equipping, and discipleship, those men are now at a place where they can make a significant impact as *nation changers*.

HUNGRY FOR HOPE

In desperate times, people are hungry for something solid to hang on to. They're eager to hear about truth and hope in Christ. Cathy first experienced this in the refugee camps in Turkey and Iraq.

While actively ministering to people's physical needs, Cathy and other aid workers were also secretly working with people who were spiritually open. Many Kurds, faced with crisis and loss of nearly everything they owned, were in a position to hear the gospel for the first time. Social pressures removed, people were no longer afraid to choose.

Cathy recalls handing out tracts as people rushed around her, asking for their own copy.

"We heard about this on the radio."

"Can I have one of those books?"

And Cathy realized the radio programs had prepared their hearts. They had heard enough of the truth that they were interested. Displaced from their homes and no longer surrounded by the heavy influence of neighbors, friends, or family, these people were desperate. They were hungry for any kind of hope.

God was always working His plan—the war just sped things up.

God is the one who prepares people's hearts. He uses all kinds of things, even heartaches and hard times. He doesn't stop war. He doesn't stop sickness. But He does use it to draw people to Himself.

IT'S NOT ALL ABOUT MEDICINE

In Sudan, as Cathy was treating patients at the hospital, she noticed that the hospital chaplain didn't have much to do. He seemed to be something of an afterthought, just waiting for people to come his way. Cathy was well aware that her patients' problems weren't only medical, so she determined to let the chaplain play a more active role.

Again, her intuition and insight got things done.

As part of her regular patient-care protocol, Cathy began sending patients to the chaplain to be prayed over. Rather than being an afterthought, the chaplain became the first line of treatment and eventually a central hub of the clinic.

Over time they added two more chaplains eager to serve God in this way. On fire for the Lord, the chaplains completely changed the dynamic of the clinic. They were bold in their faith. They had been set free from false religion and witchcraft and were not afraid to pray for physical healing and spiritual victory.

As people came to faith in Christ, they often discarded their amulets and charms. Every month the chaplains would collect them and discard them by the boxful as God revealed Himself to new believers.

Yasir's story is just one example.

When Bubba and Cathy first met this young man, he was crippled. He was completely bent over with sickly, gaunt features and haunted eyes. He walked haltingly only with the help of a stick that served as a makeshift cane. He went to the tribal witch doctor again and again, seeking help but with no results. Something of a social outcast, he started going to Bubba and Cathy's little ragtag church. He would hobble into the back, listen, and then leave immediately. Week after week and month after month, he came without interacting or engaging, seemingly in anguish for the evil to leave him.

Until one day something changed.

Approaching Bubba after church, he said, "I want you and Cathy to come to my house today. I want to show you something."

They followed him to his little hut nearby and waited while he went in. Moving slowly, he came out carrying a large pile of amulets.

"Today I want to choose to follow the Christ that you're teaching about in this church. These amulets are not helping me. I want to burn these here with you."

With hearts rejoicing and tears threatening, Bubba and Cathy placed their hands on him and prayed. They prayed for deliverance from evil spirits. They asked the Holy Spirit to be in him powerfully. They asked God to use this man to take the gospel to the hard places where the enemy is active. Then together they burned the amulets to a heap of ashes on the hard African clay.

The next Sunday, Yasir hobbled from his usual place at the back of the church to the front and asked to speak to the group. Not only did he share his story, but he preached a sermon. From that day on, he became a student of the Bible, often studying late into the night.

During the days he worked with Bubba in construction, and as he grew in spiritual maturity, it soon became obvious that he was also gaining physical strength. Each day his crippled body seemed to straighten up a little bit more.

One day he returned to the witch doctor whose help he had sought so often.

"Do you remember me?" he asked.

The last time the witch doctor had seen him, Yasir had been a bent-over cripple, desperately clinging to a crooked stick. The young man before him now stood tall, like a completely different person. The witch doctor looked at him in confusion. Yasir explained that not only was his physical appearance different, but his heart and spiritual destiny had also been changed. As he shared his testimony about how the gospel had transformed his life, others in the witch doctor's compound also heard.

One by one, many of them picked up their things and left the witch doctor's influence.

And what does this young man do now? Now he's one of those chaplains changing the dynamic at the hospital . . . because it's not only about medicine.

Word spread. (Good news always does.)

People would come to the hospital from the refugee camps, often walking past free clinics, to visit Cathy's clinic. It wasn't free. They had to pay one Sudanese pound to see a doctor.

One day Cathy asked, "Why are you willing to walk so far and pass all these free clinics to come to ours?"

Their answer? "Because you care and your prayers work and you have good medicine."

Beyond simply treating patients, Bubba and Cathy also focused on training.

Upon returning to Sudan after an evacuation, local hospital staff approached them, saying, "We're not going to let you leave until you teach us all we need to know. We've watched people die, and we don't want to go through that again. We want to know how to suture. We want to know how to deliver babies and how to take care of burns."

This reinforces a trend we're seeing in medical missions in many countries. Western missionaries can have a big impact by focusing on training local people. In many ways it's equipping the saints to do the work of ministry, albeit with a medical slant. Educated, trained native medical professionals and spiritual leaders can totally change the dynamic in the hospital and in their communities. It starts with stories like Yasir's.

RUNNING TOWARD HARD THINGS

Why have Bubba and Cathy spent the last several decades in these hard places when they could have done any number of other, less difficult things? Cathy points to the world map as if the answer is clear. If you mark out the areas of the world that are unreached or underserved in terms of healthcare and overlay that with a map of areas of the world that are unreached by the gospel, there's a significant overlap. In the places of the world where there's a dearth of healthcare workers, there's also a spiritual darkness.

When they were first married, Bubba and Cathy had a vision of a spark that started small and spread outward, pushing back evil and pushing the gospel outward, all the way to the sea. They have lived their lives as little sparks spreading out across both of those maps. And those little sparks have started a big fire.

How have they done it? The grace of God, of course. But Cathy also feels like her chaotic childhood uniquely prepared her to deal with upheaval and difficulty. Her years of war in Iraq prepared her for living in war-torn Sudan. It may be hard to fathom, but Bubba says you just get used to it. "After a while you don't even realize it's a hard life anymore."

This is a pretty telling statement, considering Bubba and Cathy had lost everything they owned *four times* due to evacuation from Sudan and other rough places. They became so used to the upheaval that they began to get annoyed by the calls to evacuate. They had work to do and didn't want to leave!

Cathy recalls being more angry than afraid. They both believe if God's plan is for them to live, He'll let them live. If not, they're going to die, and they know where they're going. They don't have qualms about that. It's literally courage under fire.

In what would become their last days on the ground in Sudan, Cathy was angry. It was Christmas, and the fighting was heavy. Outside their courtyard, the bullets were flying as they got caught between the battle lines between the refugee militia group and a militia group from the local community. The desert sun was relentless as they hunkered down for several days without electricity, only venturing to their outside toilets when there was a lull in the fighting.

Sweating, listening to the chattering of machine guns in the distance, with flies buzzing around and so many questions swirling in her head, Cathy couldn't help but feel frustrated.

What a waste. There's work to be done here, lives are being lost unnecessarily, and for goodness' sake, it's Christmas!

During all this chaos, they thankfully had constant internet access via their solar power. It soon became clear that this wasn't a small skirmish and they would once again have to make plans to evacuate. They were in touch with a UN contact who said they'd send someone to get Bubba and Cathy and over thirty other workers out of the country.

Time went by, but the UN convoy never came. Not surprisingly, Bubba took matters into his own hands. He contacted another mission organization about a plane. His level head and training in disaster-assistance response proved invaluable to the team of frightened coworkers and visitors.

The messages went back and forth over several hours before the call finally came.

"We've got three planes, and we're coming in to get you. It will be tight, but we'll get you and your team out. After twenty minutes on the ground, we're going wheels up. So be ready. Twenty minutes max on the ground. It's not safe to stay any longer than that."

In a mad dash, Cathy and Bubba rounded up their team. It was going to be tight, so each person could only pack a twenty-kilo bag (about forty-four pounds). How do you pack up a life in a forty-four pound bag? Not knowing if they'd be back, they scrambled to collect the most important things. Everything else would have to stay behind.

Following evacuation protocols (this wasn't their first rodeo—not that that made it any easier), they quickly paid their local staff and said a hasty, tear-filled goodbye to friends. Wrapping things up as well as they could in such a short time, and with prayers for protection on their lips, they headed out.

Since the UN convoy did not show up to help them drive to the UN compound, the staff formed a convoy of their own. As they raced to the airstrip, they saw homes destroyed and burned, and some of their neighbors who had been shot and killed. As Cathy drove by the clinic, she never figured it would be the last time she would see it.

True to their word, the mission aviation team landed the three planes, one after the other, to scoop up the missionaries. Engines screaming, people running, tears streaming, dust flying, the aviation team loaded up the missionaries and their meager belongings.

In and out, twenty minutes.

As the planes flew up and over the disastrous scene, Cathy's heart broke. Their neighborhood was dead quiet—everyone had run into the bush to escape the fighting. Even the refugee camp near the clinic was empty and deserted. All had fled.

So many years had been spent there. So many had found hope in Christ. The church they had helped start . . . So many amazing things had happened. And it was all gone. Why? Why would God let this happen?

They had no way of knowing this would be their last view of Sudan. And they had no way of knowing in those traumatic, heartbreaking days that they would continue to see God move in Sudan . . . through the people they had trained and discipled.

As you can imagine, this exit from Sudan was traumatic. Their mission organization urged Bubba and Cathy to take some time away for crisis debriefing, counseling, and recuperation. Then they asked the couple to consider a new place of service. Another hard place.

Maybe even the hardest place so far.

At the time of this writing, Bubba and Cathy have lived in Jordan for the past six years. She works in a clinic, and the two of them together minister in the community. Jordan is hard in different ways than other places they've been. Unlike in the desperate, chaotic places they'd been before, they've now been in this dry, dusty, relatively safe country for six years, and *only two people have come to Christ.*

In Jordan, the challenge is to remain faithful without seeing results. When I spoke with them, I could sense the heaviness in their hearts. They don't doubt God's calling to be there, but it takes its toll when you can't see the fruit of your labor. And without a community of believers around them for support and encouragement, they know this might not be a long-term assignment.

But they are living out what God spoke to them years ago:

I want you to get on My coattail and just follow. Hang on, because it's going to be a wild ride.

INSIGHT, WISDOM, AND TAKEAWAYS

As Bubba and Cathy consider what God has next for them, they are excited about moving into a mentoring role. With the overlapping world maps of spiritually and medically unreached people at the forefront of their minds, they are eager to raise up a new generation of missionaries who are completely committed to following God to the hard places. After nearly two decades of doing just that, they've learned a thing or two about persistence and following God's leading.

For the next generation of missionaries, they offer this advice: Stay close to the Lord. Know what you believe. Spend time allowing yourself to be discipled. Don't make decisions using your own wisdom. Wait to hear from God. Seek counsel. When you encounter culture shock in your first months in a new place (and you will), when you find yourself mired in disagreements with coworkers, or when you have to face your first evacuation, remember that God has *called* you and He is always faithful.

And one more thing—a *called* person is dangerous to the enemy. Go be dangerous.

CHAPTER 3

KATHERINE WELCH

RELENTLESS

If there's one word that describes Katherine Welch, it's *relentless*. With a pixie-cut mop of unruly hair, kind blue eyes, and a ready smile, that word might not immediately spring to mind, but get her talking about the work she's done for over two decades, and those bright eyes turn flinty and intense—relentless.

Like many of the stories in this book, hers follows an unconventional path.

She didn't set out to practice jungle medicine in Thailand. She didn't intend to teach Chinese doctors pediatric medicine or rescue orphaned Chinese babies from malnutrition. Nor did she imagine she would dedicate her life to ministering to sex trafficking victims. She didn't intend to start Relentless, an organization whose mission is to "seek liberty through health at the intersection of health and justice so that all abused, exploited, or trafficked people receive quality, trauma-informed care and are empowered to thrive in robust wellness for the rest of their lives."

All that would come, but only later.

Because as a young college student, Katherine didn't even intend to be a doctor.

She began her studies planning to become an athletic trainer or physical therapist. But as she studied, she discovered that she loved all of the human body, not just the parts physical therapy focuses on. And several professors saw something in her, saying often, "Katherine, maybe you should be a doctor."

Not one to overthink things, Katherine agreed. She has that kind of go-to mentality that helps her make a decision and take action.

She pivoted, graduated medical school, and took her board certifications.

While most newly minted doctors would have sighed with relief that the gauntlet was behind them and started enjoying a six-figure salary, Katherine took a different approach: she boarded a plane to Thailand to work along the war-torn borders of Burma (now Myanmar) populated with refugee camps.

It wasn't a random choice. Katherine had been there before.

I DON'T WANT TO DO WHAT EVERYONE ELSE IS DOING

During medical school, students were encouraged to travel abroad and experience medicine there. Students usually went to Africa, Asia, and Europe. But when Thailand came up and Katherine's advisor mentioned his connection to Dr. Phil McDaniel and said they'd never sent a student there before, those flinty eyes sparked to life.

That's where she wanted to go—Kwai River Christian Hospital in Thailand.

Those two months in Thailand were the most amazing months of her life. The tropical warmth, the lush green landscape, and the richness of the village and community life drew Katherine in. Like every other part of her journey, Katherine jumped in with two feet. Though her training was in pediatrics, she quickly found herself practicing tropical medicine and assisting with surgery.

Being a "jungle doctor" is exactly what it sounds like. It's as far away from the fluorescent lights, sterilized instruments, and cutting-edge technology of a first-world hospital as can be. But her can-do attitude and the wise guidance of Dr. McDaniel gave her confidence. She was in her element. She wasn't reckless with people's lives or arrogant about her abilities—she knew how much she didn't know. But even as a medical student, there was something she could do. The doctors and the patients trusted her. Their patience and her enthusiasm together provided an excellent learning environment.

The big picture focus was simple: keep the humans alive. For the most part, the patients who came to the hospital did not have a family doctor to give them any kind of regular medical care. In such a remote region, there simply wasn't a doctor available. If people came to the hospital, it was because they were sick or injured. Many traveled a great distance—sometimes for weeks— seeking treatment for fevers, chronic diseases, and traumatic accident injuries. As the referral center for the refugee camps, Katherine's hospital was the last stop for most people.

If the doctors at Kwai River couldn't help them, then there was no help.

The need was overwhelming, but Katherine found that they were not overwhelmed. They simply did what they could in the hours of the day. Not everyone is wired to do this kind of work, under these circumstances, but Katherine quickly knew she was. She felt that she could actually make a difference. She felt like God had made her for this kind of purpose, for this kind of hard work. *If not her, then who?*

Because of that two-month residency experience in Thailand, Katherine knew when it came time to start her career that she would continue to follow a different path. She would not do what most other medical students did.

Turning down several attractive fellowship offers, as soon as she passed her board certifications, she packed her bags and headed back to Thailand. She wanted to see what it was like long-term, to dig in after the honeymoon experience of those first two months.

Did she have a plan? A step-by-step itinerary for her career trajectory? No. She simply began.

Her only plan was to be there for as long as it took to do the work.

PASSION AND PURPOSE

Katherine didn't have a plan, but she was confident that God did. As a young person, Katherine hadn't been challenged to actively live out her faith until university and medical school. During those years, as she was receiving career training, she was also experiencing exponential spiritual growth. She admits that her initial motivation to go to Thailand might have been more along the lines of philanthropic adventure rather than spiritual calling, but it didn't take long for her to become convinced that God had placed her in Asia for His purposes.

Several years into her work in Thailand, busy stitching up lacerations, treating skin diseases, and delivering babies, Katherine got an interesting request from colleagues in a different part of the country.

"Hey, Katherine. Would you be interested in going with us to the red-light district in Bangkok? We're working with some women who need medical care, but they are reluctant to see a doctor. They need treatment, and we could use your expertise. Can you help us?"

Deep into the hospital work in Thailand, Katherine couldn't imagine where that simple request would lead. She didn't know anything about the anti-trafficking medical ministry. She didn't even understand the context of their question.

Why would people in the red-light district be reluctant to see a doctor?

But true to form, her can-do attitude kicked in. Here was a way she could help. Here was another thing she could do. Working with her colleagues in Bangkok, her eyes were opened to a whole new area of medical need. She discovered that people working in the sex trade are often shunned, shamed, and mistreated—even by healthcare workers. As she learned more and more, Katherine's heart was stirred to help fight this evil.

Over the next several years, Katherine's medical work took her to various locations in China, back to Thailand, and even to Europe. No matter the location, her day-to-day workload varied, but always there was a pull toward ministering to those caught in human trafficking.

As a pediatrician, her day job involved nursing babies back to health, teaching Chinese doctors pediatric medicine, and doing compassionate care in orphanages. But her true passion became the work that she was doing with the anti-trafficking organizations.

Katherine began traveling throughout China and to Malaysia, Singapore, Cambodia, and Thailand. On these trips she would learn and help, letting God use her as He would.

"Help me help You help these women," she said again and again. "I'm a doctor, and I want to learn."

As she was learning, she was sharing the love of Christ. Working with the anti-trafficking organizations, she began seeing patients at health clinics in the red-light districts. The clinics would run throughout the night, often starting at five in the evening and going until two or three in the morning. Or she would visit a drop-in center for boys who were trafficked for sex or a shelter for pregnant women and premature babies. They offered free HIV testing and any other healthcare that was needed. She would prescribe medication that they could get over the counter and offer treatment suggestions.

As heartbreaking as it sounds, Katherine was in her element. She simply did what she could do, relentless in her pursuit of protection and care for the oppressed.

Along the way, Katherine also found herself teaching as well as treating. People in the anti-trafficking organizations thought she'd merely help with basic healthcare but soon found she could reach much deeper needs. The chronic pain of this traumatic lifestyle affected more than just physical health. From sexually transmitted diseases to bizarre attitudes that developed as a result of severe, ongoing trauma, the physiological and the psychological were intimately connected and Katherine began to change the narrative.

In regular society, Katherine observed a general apathy toward the treatment of those in this industry. Because of religious beliefs around karma, the attitudes of the locals often went like, *Why should I care? These people obviously deserve this.* And even among Christians, there was an attitude of disgust, repulsion, and a reluctance to provide medical care, let alone compassion. *They're getting what they deserve.*

MORE THAN MEDICINE

Katherine obviously does not share that sentiment. She has dedicated her professional life to bringing respect, quality care, dignity, and a chance at a better life to survivors of abuse, exploitation, and human trafficking.

From the jungles of Thailand to the red-light districts and orphanages in China, she's seen enough pain and human suffering to last a lifetime. And more than prescribing medicines, performing surgeries, and offering bandages, Katherine knows it's the hearts and souls that matter.

At one evening clinic for boys in Bangkok, Katherine placed her stethoscope on a boy's chest, his dull brown eyes gazing at nothing in the middle distance, not meeting hers.

"Breathe in. Hold it. Again."

Looking directly into his eyes, she told him his heart was fine. His heart was healthy.

And then she prayed aloud, "Dear Jesus, please speak to his good heart. Show him your love, no matter the shame and pain he might be feeling now. Heal his body, but more than that, speak to his heart."

Katherine knew that the young boy she was treating would only go right back to the streets after he saw her at the clinic. But as she did for all her patients—this boy being only one among thousands—she prayed God would go with him. Because this was not just about medicine. It was also a spiritual battle.

Jesus promised that in this world, we would have trouble. And there was so much trouble in Asia. Though Katherine is known for her never-quit attitude, there were definitely days when she wanted to quit, turn in her missionary card, and be done with it all. Knowing someone was going back to the life of prostitution after being treated and told of a different way of life. Hearing someone had died or had run off or was experiencing distressing PTSD episodes. Some days it just seemed there were so many unanswered questions and so much futility.

They say you cannot go near a fire and not expect to get burned. Katherine felt the burn of evil every day in China, usually in physical ways—sickness and depression.

Am I doing any good? What's the use of this? Do I even believe in the goodness of God anymore?

These questions would plague her in the night. Torturous evil thoughts, feelings of despair, and unbidden temptations all swirling, she would call on the name of Jesus aloud. Other times she would call a friend to talk through the long hours of the night, or she would sing.

One night Katherine started to cry out but found she could not open her mouth. It was as if her face had melted and she physically could not speak. In her head and heart, she continued to cry out, repeating everything she knew to be true—about God and His good work and about herself and the work He was empowering her to do—until the attack passed.

After some time in China, she began to see a pattern.

It's clinic day? Of course you feel sick. This is from the enemy. Are you discouraged? Of course. It's because you shared the love of Jesus with someone in bondage. The enemy wants to keep her in bondage!

As she traveled around, Katherine was always aware of the enemy.

Part of being relentless is persevering through struggle and spiritual oppression. And when the right person is in the right place at the right time and taps into the power of the living God, amazing things happen. And amazing organizations are birthed.

BE RELENTLESS

Today Katherine is asking herself what it looks like for a doctor to devote all her time, energy, and funding to work at the intersection of health and human trafficking in Southeast Asia and beyond.

In 2011, she founded Relentless, a nonprofit organization focused on just that. The organization holds clinics for exploited people in red-light districts as well as in residential aftercare programs. They also focus on educating those who work with survivors of human trafficking about the mental and physical impacts that come with this kind of trauma and help anti-trafficking organizations develop a stronger healthcare component to their interventions.

Because of her years of experience and travels, Katherine has developed a keen sense of the needs of the exploited, the exploiter, and those who care for survivors. With compassion and tenacity, Katherine continues to allow God to use her.

Just as she learned so many years ago in Thailand, it's not about the impact one person can have. It's not about Dr. Katherine. She knows it could have been anyone, but God placed her in the midst of a global community doing His work. She said yes, other people said yes, and God created the impact.

God is in the business of transformation and reconciliation— for all of us.

INSIGHT, WISDOM, AND TAKEAWAYS

Grow in God. Develop a deep trust in Him. Then do what you like and are good at, and wait to see how God will use it. It might be in ways that you can't even imagine. And it's okay if all the steps are not neatly lined out, one after the other. God has to move each of us in some way. Take the first step, and let God be creative with what He does. As you walk with Him, you'll develop that deep trust—in His goodness and His plan.

After over twenty years of following God's lead, Dr. Katherine Welch knows, if you're going with God, you're not going to fail. No matter what.

CHAPTER 4

CAROL SPEARS

CHANGES

C arol Spears has learned quite a bit about winding paths in the last thirty years. But as a young adult, her life path seemed pretty straight.

Carol's pastor father and teacher mother loved Jesus and taught Carol to love him too, but Carol had no plans to follow her parents' career choices. She was not interested in a service profession. She wanted to go into the business world. She set her sights on achieving worldly success and climbing the corporate ladder . . . straight to the top. No winding path necessary.

A degree in math and computer science led to a career in the telecommunications industry and a move from her home state of Alabama to New Jersey. In hindsight now, Carol jokingly refers to that work-related relocation as her first cross-cultural experience. There were more to come, but she had no idea at the time.

Carol excelled at her work, and as she focused on her career, she lost sight of things that had once been important. She no longer walked with the Lord and made choices that she now looks back on with regret. She was busy and successful. She began an executive MBA program . . . just another step on that straight path to the top.

But the Lord has plans for you too.

In the midst of her worldly living, career success, and studying for an MBA, Carol received a letter from a dear friend. They had been close since the age of ten. They kept in touch though their lives had taken wildly different paths. Her friend and her husband had gone to seminary and then been called as missionaries and were living in Nigeria. She and Carol sent letters back and forth by airmail (this was before email and social media made overseas communication so much easier).

One day Carol opened the envelope with the foreign stamps and was stunned to read the words, "Carol, who are you? I don't understand what's happened to you, but I don't think you're someone that I can call my best friend anymore."

To say those words were devastating would be an understatement.

Carol's friend was going through some rough times of suffering in her early years of missionary service. And Carol, her best friend, was too busy to write or call—*very* caught up in her *very* important life and her *very* important job.

This letter from a hurting friend half a world away was what the Lord used to break Carol's heart. She got on her knees and repented . . . and then stayed up all night trying to call Nigeria to reconcile with her friend. Not only did they restore their friendship, but they soon began making plans for Carol to visit her in Nigeria.

In June of that year, Carol graduated from the MBA program, rejoicing that she'd never have to go to school again. They say man plans and God laughs.

One month later, she was in Nigeria. Her friend worked as a nurse assisting surgeons in the operating room and at a children's home with children and new mothers—actually saving human lives. Carol's eyes were opened. Here was work that made a difference in the kingdom. Her successful life back in America, staying up all night to prepare a presentation for an executive, didn't compare to what they were doing here.

And Carol had a feeling that the straight path to the top of the corporate world was about to take an abrupt turn. While in Nigeria, she sensed that the Lord was directing her to return to America . . . and go to medical school.

A LATE START IS RIGHT ON TIME

How do you start a second career in your thirties? One step at a time.

The first time Carol tentatively mentioned this new calling to anyone other than her long-time friend, it was to a group of doctors sitting around her friend's kitchen table in Nigeria.

She said, "I feel like God's calling me to medical school. I have no idea how this could even work. I don't have the funds to do it. My parents don't either. Could God really be calling me to this? How? How would I do this?"

And those doctors started throwing out idioms.

"A journey of a thousand miles starts with one step at a time."

"How do you eat an elephant? One bite at a time."

And that joking, tongue-in-cheek counsel set the tone. Indeed, one step, one bite at a time, she returned to the United States and began to follow a new path.

At the time Carol was living in Atlanta, Georgia, working for AT&T. Everybody told her she should keep quiet about her plans because she was in a program for corporate advancement where she could move up the ladder and be promoted.

Everyone said, "You can't tell them that you're thinking of making a complete change."

But she didn't know what else to do, so, scared to death of his reaction, she told her division manager.

To her surprise, he put down his pen, removed his glasses, and looked her directly in the eyes.

"Carol, I am so envious of you. You really know what it is you want to do."

And even though this was a significant deviation from the expected path, her supervisor ended up being very supportive.

Carol moved to Birmingham, Alabama, to take a lower-level job so she could start night classes—labs and prerequisites. Then came the MCAT, and application and acceptance to medical school. At the age of thirty-four, Carol Spears, MBA, started medical school at University of Alabama–Birmingham with the goal of becoming Carol Spears, MD.

For the next several years, the path was pretty clear. The set steps were laid out; she simply had to complete them.

Carol didn't know what type of medicine she wanted to specialize in when she began, but she found herself drawn to surgery. In spite of it taking a longer time to complete the training and many advising against it as an older student, it was what she loved, and she felt like the Lord was leading her in that direction.

After medical school, Carol matched with the University of Kentucky for her general surgical residency. She thrived there and wanted to finish on track with her class. However, through a series of God-orchestrated events, after her third year of training, Carol ended up taking a year out of her Kentucky residency training program and spending a year at a mission hospital in rural Kenya.

That would be a pivotal year in her new career path.

During the year at Tenwek Hospital, God began moving Carol's intentions from short-term medical missions trips to full-time, long-term overseas service. He was calling her to be a career missionary.

After that year in Kenya, Carol returned for the two final years of residency in the USA, and then it was decision time.

What was Carol going to do with all this training? And what about the mountain of educational debt that she needed to start repaying? She didn't think she wanted to stay in America. After all, it was in the context of medical missions that she had started this journey.

MedSend came through for the medical debt.

And her heart continued to be drawn to Tenwek Hospital in Kenya. She had experience there. They were interested in her coming back. So she stepped out.

"God, please just shut the doors if that's not the right place. And fling them wide open if it is."

And of course, that's what God did.

And at age forty-six—fourteen and a half years after she felt the first call of God directing her to a career change—Dr. Carol Spears moved to Kenya as a full-time missionary surgeon.

KENYA

Carol threw herself into the work there and fell in love with Kenya and her patients. She says she tells people to be very careful when they visit Africa, because the bug will bite you. When you land on African soil, you're going to fall in love with the place. It might not happen for everybody, but it did for Carol.

By the time she moved to Kenya, Carol had returned to Nigeria a few times, and even though East and West Africa are completely different, her love for the places and the patients was the same. God gave her a love for the people of Kenya and a desire to see them grow deeper in their faith or come to know Jesus if they didn't know him.

Carol calls Tenwek Hospital in the beautiful Rift Valley of Kenya "Africa for Beginners." It's a comfortable place to live with Western-style homes and food. But there are differences.

As a general surgeon, she had to be ready for whatever would come her way on a given day—gynecological, vascular, endocrine, colorectal, plastic surgery. There weren't a lot of options for referring to specialists in the early days. And even if there was somewhere they could send patients, they would often not be able to go either because of expense or difficulty getting there.

Tenwek served as a referral center for surgical oncology. They received patients from Somalia, Uganda, and other countries because of the groundbreaking work one of her colleagues was doing in treating esophageal cancer. They also treated a lot of gastric and prostate cancer.

Orthopedic trauma surgeries were a daily occurrence. In the United States, surgeons refer to the "knife and gun club" when it comes to traumatic injuries. In Kenya, they call it the *"panga* and *rungu* club." A *panga* is a long machete, and a *rungu* is a club-like mallet. Both serve utilitarian purposes in daily life, but when wielded as weapons, they can create a lot of damage that requires surgical treatment. They also saw quite a few injuries from arrows and wild animals, including buffalos and cows.

More than just treating their ailments, they also want to minister to patients' souls.

At Tenwek Hospital, the motto is, "We treat, Jesus heals."

BUILDING FOR THE FUTURE

Part of Carol's initial uncertainty about going to Tenwek full-time was because the hospital already had two general surgeons. Shouldn't she go somewhere with a greater need? But in time, God made it clear that Tenwek was where He wanted her, and it soon became obvious that she was an integral part of the team there.

When deciding to pursue medical training, Carol wasn't necessarily thinking about training others. Her mother had been a teacher, and following in her footsteps never appealed to Carol. But as a resident at Tenwek years earlier, Carol had been introduced to the Pan-African Academy of Christian Surgeons (PAACS), a nondenominational, multinational service organization training African physicians to become surgeons who are willing to remain in Africa to meet the significant need for medical care on the continent. PAACS also disciples these surgical residents to share the gospel and love of Jesus Christ with their patients. Carol's heart was captured with the passion of wanting to see talented young men and women be able to be trained in their own country with a Christian focus.

And the numbers from PAACS were staggering: the number of physicians or surgeons per capita in most African countries is so much lower than in America or other places around the world. The training for doctors was limited, and if they had to leave their countries to get it, many never returned. The brain drain was real.

Carol and her surgical colleagues had a shared vision for a surgical residency program at Tenwek. And one year after she arrived, they began the program. Carol became a teacher and also something like a mom and encourager to these young residents.

The process wasn't easy. It didn't happen overnight. The concept of being able to use a Christian mission hospital as a training institution was new. It took some work to get the various government authorities to agree that their program would, in fact, be comparable or even better than the existing programs at the government hospitals. Carol and her colleagues worked long hours to define the residency program—including a curriculum, exams, and a plan for practical training.

And then the next question: Who would be the first to try the program? To have a residency program, you need residents. Tenwek Hospital was already training and teaching in other areas, but would anyone take a chance on this new surgical residency program?

One young resident was thinking about pediatrics or cardiology, but when they asked if she'd consider surgery instead, she agreed to be a "guinea pig for Jesus." She didn't know as she started her training in 2008 if this residency program was ever going to fully come to fruition. She had no guarantee that it would be accredited by the medical authorities in Kenya. But she was willing. And then they added another trainee, and with two residents, their program was off the ground.

The first few years were intense. Not only were the surgeons creating a new program, but they were also still taking calls and often up all night, all without a well-trained surgery resident by their side. But as the program matured, it got better and better, and it became a joy to be able to pour into the training of these young doctors. And they were able to study the Bible and pray and worship together as part of training a wholehearted Christian surgeon.

They all had lessons to learn, and God was working in all of their lives to teach and grow and refine them. By the time the first two residents graduated, they had affiliation with the College of Surgeons of East, Central, and Southern Africa (COSECSA) and the approval of the Kenya Medical and Dental Board. What a joy it was to know that those first two graduates would be able to take their exams and do all their qualifications and be fully recognized as surgeons.

Early on, as they began envisioning the surgical residency program, Carol and her colleagues turned to Psalm 127:1 as their guiding light:

Unless the LORD builds the house, the builders labor in vain.

And as a bookend, Psalm 118:23:

The LORD has done this, and it is marvelous in our eyes.

They used these two verses from Psalms back-to-back to simply say, "God built this." They knew from the beginning that was the only way it would be successful.

Six years later, as they graduated the first two residents, they saw that the Lord was faithful. He had done it.

Tenwek Hospital had two new, top-notch general surgeons—pursuing excellence and serving God in their own country.

YOU ARE MY BELOVED

In the first difficult years of the residency program, Carol came face-to-face with her own limitations and doubts. In the early days, there was so much to do and so few people to do them. The long days and nights, interpersonal complications, and logistical difficulties were taking their toll. The residency program seemed as if it was about to implode. Something inside Carol cracked. She was burned out, desperate, and felt like a complete failure.

I tried to come and serve You, Lord, and do my best, and it's just not working out.

She was so discouraged that she could not continue in her work for several weeks. In those weeks of resting and seeking the Lord, God met her in a way that would influence her work and ministry for the rest of her life.

God impressed upon her this truth: *Carol, you are My beloved. It's not about what you can do. I don't need you to do My work. You are My beloved, and I want you to* be *with Me.*

That lesson of learning to rest in Him and to draw strength from Him has proved valuable again and again. And after that point, Carol says her priorities shifted. Yes, work and the residency program were still important, but they weren't everything.

A HEART FOR MUSLIM WOMEN

As Carol learned to trust and rest in the Lord, and as the residency program matured, she began to feel a restlessness in her soul. There were more people involved in the program with fresh ideas and new energy. Knowing the work would continue on with the people God was providing, Carol began to wonder if God had a new place for her. Was God calling her somewhere else?

Carol loved all her patients but was especially drawn to Muslim women with their covered faces and mysterious lifestyles behind their veils. During Carol's year-long residency at Tenwek, she cared for a Muslim woman who had traveled for two days from near the border of Somalia seeking treatment for esophageal cancer. She was admitted and had to stay in the hospital for a long time and get some nutrition before she could be operated on. The surgery to remove the cancer was successful, and ultimately, she was able to go home.

But she'd been there long enough that Carol had formed a relationship with her. And in her fledgling, inept way, Carol wanted to share her faith with her. Despite the differences between Islam and Christianity, the one thing both religions have in common is the belief in prayer. So Carol prayed for her and then said, "I would like to give you something."

She knew it was doubtful that the woman would be able to read the *Good News Bible* in English, but she prayed somebody in her village or family would read it to her.

Over the years, this woman's face stayed in Carol's mind. Several years later, when Carol was back in Kenya as a full-time surgeon, the woman's cancer recurred, and she was re-hospitalized in Tenwek. Eventually, she did pass away . . . but her life and death had an impact on Carol that would last for years to come. Carol says, "She planted the seed in my heart for Muslim women."

Carol also had a fifty-one-year-old Muslim patient with a cleft lip. She had been divorced and driven out of the support of other Muslim people because of it. And she had turned to working as a sex worker to earn school fees to send her kids to school. A local church contacted Carol.

"Would you consider performing surgery on this woman?"

Of course, she did. And again, Carol's heart was stirred with love for Muslim women.

Knowing the residency program was in good hands, Carol could have been looking ahead to retirement. It might have seemed relatively easy to finish out her ministry years in the comfort of the familiar. But Carol has never been one to take the easy route. She has not shied away from making big changes that others wouldn't even consider, whether it's a career change or a location change.

And so, with serving Muslim women at the forefront of her mind and heart, Carol began the difficult process of pulling up roots in Kenya, a place she had loved and called home for fourteen years.

After visiting several different places, at the age of fifty-nine, Carol traded the familiarity of Africa for the unknowns of the Middle East.

Carol took a position as a general surgeon consultant at a hospital in Arabia. The hospital is one of only two mission hospitals on the Arabian Peninsula. It was founded in 1960 by two Christian medical missionaries who were invited to come by local sheikhs. The sheikhs had received healthcare at Christian missions in Oman and Bahrain. They were convinced that these American Christian doctors were doing good things, and they wanted that for their own people.

At the time, about half of the children were dying before age one, and 30 percent of the women were dying in childbirth. The sheikhs recognized that if something didn't change, their population was not going to make it. The two Christians doctors were open about their faith, they loved the people well, and they practiced good medical and surgical care. They won the favor of that local community and the royal family.

Today this hospital declares that their purpose is to honor God by providing whole-person medical care with the love and compassion of Jesus Christ. Though they serve everyone, it is primarily a maternity and pediatric hospital, not a surgery hospital, so Carol's days look much different than they did in Kenya.

Carol finds that though she is providing medical care, her ministry is primarily relational—with the women she serves and the people she works with. The hospital employs people from forty different countries, and only a fraction are practicing Christians. This environment is a challenge, but Carol says people always respond to love and compassion and kindness.

And when she feels discouraged, Carol remembers the lesson God so vividly taught her in Kenya. He doesn't need her to reach people. God simply calls her to be faithful.

INSIGHT, WISDOM, AND TAKEAWAYS

Shine brightly. Show love and compassion. Whether it's in the Middle East, Africa, or some other place, people respond to kindness. Medicine is a marvelous tool to provide physical healing and point people to spiritual healing. Carol knows as well as anyone that it can be hard to shine brightly, especially when you're running behind and everyone around you is upset and plans aren't going as you anticipated.

For new missionaries—be sure of your calling. Is it Jesus calling you to do something? Is he the one giving you your passion, your dream, your desire, your calling? If so, then hold on to that when discouragements come. He is faithful, and he will do what he says.

Every single person that God uses has times of despair and disappointment. Times may come when you don't feel like you're doing anything right. Most missionaries go to the field with dreams and aspirations and ambitions, and then when it doesn't turn out as you thought, you feel like you're failing and disappointing God. You change your whole life to pursue your highest calling and then find you're not doing a good job of it.

So when you come to those points—maybe multiple times over the course of your career—trust God. Take heart that He is the one doing the work. And stay connected to Jesus.

The light of Christ *will* illuminate dark places—in your own heart and in the world around you. When you let His light shine brightly *through* you, He gets the glory and you get to be the spark the world needs.

CHAPTER 5

CATHERINE HODGE

P E R S P E C T I V E

C atherine Hodge was fascinated with missionary slideshows. It wasn't the cool thing to do, and as a teenager, she tried to hide it from her friends. But she couldn't help it. Every year her Baptist church in Florida held a weeklong missions conference. And every year Catherine could not wait to see the presentations from missionaries from far-flung places like Papua New Guinea or remote villages in Africa.

Year after year, she heard the stories and saw the photos, and year after year, her heart was stirred. As a teenager she was challenged by this weekly conference to think more deeply about what she was going to do with her life. The years of missionary stories all came together when she was seventeen. The way she saw it, she could devote her adult life and career toward trying to further the gospel in whatever form the Lord would direct, or she could live for herself—have a comfortable life and be a Christian on the side.

That year Catherine made a commitment to devote herself to "full-time ministry." Though her definition of full-time ministry has become more nuanced since then, at the time she saw only two options: preacher or missionary. And since her denomination doesn't ordain women ministers, missionary it was.

With the spiritual commitment settled, Catherine began to explore what being a missionary could look like. She loved traveling and adventure. She wanted to share the gospel. How those two things might blend, she wasn't sure. During this time Catherine also found herself getting in trouble in her high school—in trouble for reading too far ahead in the anatomy and physiology textbook.

So, she thought, *maybe medicine?*

After four years of undergraduate studies, she applied to multiple medical schools and was accepted at one . . . then wait-listed, then dropped.

In what she described as an "Isaac moment," she cried out to the Lord, "Did You bring me all this way and plant this dream in my heart only to ask me to sacrifice it now?"

Then late in the med school interview season, she got a surprising interview request with the University of Miami. Catherine had her doubts. First of all, it was a private school, which meant it would be very expensive. And second, Miami? How would a wannabe missionary ever fit in there?

To her surprise, and in God's good providence, she soon found out that her preconceived notions were way off. The school, because of its proximity to Cuba, Haiti, and Central America, had a significant focus on global health. They weren't approaching global healthcare from a Christian perspective, but they already had multiple established international programs and partnerships in place.

And when the university interviewers heard Catherine's story and her interest in practicing medicine abroad, they said, "You're just the kind of student we want," and accepted her right away.

Catherine loved medical school and settled into family medicine. She enjoyed every rotation she was on, and family medicine allowed for that variety. She met her husband, Dave, and they married when she graduated from medical school.

As a couple, Catherine says they didn't have a specific call to missions but rather a sense of freedom. Passionate about the gospel and about healthcare, she knew God had put it in her heart to serve abroad. Many people feel they can't leave America and go, but she could, and so she should. She loves it. Dave is an adventurous person, and as a new believer, he felt like every Christian was called to be involved in missions in some way, either as goers, senders, or supporters. He really liked Catherine, so together they pursued medical missions. A dream three-year residency at In His Image Family Medicine in Oklahoma, missions conferences, overseas rotations, and connections with other missionaries fanned the flames in their hearts.

It was time to move to Africa.

FIRST LESSON IN FLEXIBILITY

One of the themes that comes through again and again with missionaries I talk to is the need for flexibility. Very seldom are the working conditions perfect, the supplies adequate, or the relationships problem-free. Catherine and Dave learned this even before they arrived in Malawi.

Three weeks before they and their one-year-old child were scheduled to arrive, for reasons out of their control and that they didn't fully understand, the arrangement with the hospital where they were headed fell through. They had tickets in hand, they were fully financially funded, and had, in fact, already shipped a container with all their personal belongings.

What now, Lord?

The questions swirled around them.

Convinced that God was still directing them to Malawi, they scrambled to contact all the mission hospitals in the country. They were understandably met with skepticism by most. After all, if the hospital they had planned to go to rejected them, they must be the problem, right?

But one listened.

Nkhoma Hospital, a 107-year-old mission hospital in the Lilongwe District of Malawi, reached out. They didn't make any promises but encouraged the Hodges to keep their flights and come and see if they could create a good partnership. Catherine saw it as a good sign that the hospital did not react in desperation but that they also were cautious. Both sides needed to check out the other.

After one week in a guesthouse, all parties were in favor of the arrangement, so the Hodges signed a contract and moved into the only available house in the mission compound. Initially disappointed in the loss of the first location, they soon became grateful for the hiccup in plans.

The Nkhoma compound is large and open with Malawian neighbors. It's been a great place for their children to grow up in freedom and relative safety. It's a fit that they could not have anticipated. Not only did they learn the importance of flexibility, but also the realization, again, that if a door closes, many times the Lord has something in mind that is much better.

Catherine began to thrive in her new role.

Founded by a Dutch South African missionary in a single hut to treat people's wounds, Nkhoma Hospital had grown into a three-hundred-bed hospital—a significant growth, but still lacking in trained personnel. When Catherine arrived in 2014, she was one of only two other expatriate doctors. At the time of this writing, there are three Malawian specialist doctors—a surgeon, a family medicine physician, and an ophthalmologist—and ten more in training.

Catherine very soon found herself flexing her flexibility muscle in her work as well. As a resident, she had had a lot of experience working with very sick adults. She'd done a pediatrics rotation, but that wasn't her area of expertise. So what did the hospital need? Help in pediatrics. Terrified, Catherine agreed . . . and entered into the darkest, hardest six months of her life.

Six weeks pregnant and with a one-year-old at home, for the first time, she was watching kids die—kids often the same age as her own. The guilt and sorrow was overwhelming. Why was she here if she couldn't save lives? In such a low-resource setting, the losses were at a level she'd never experienced before, and it took its toll on her heart.

GUITAR CALLUSES AND PERSPECTIVE

When Catherine went home on her first furlough to give birth to her second child, she was unable to speak about her life in Nkhoma without crying. When a kind supporter asked how she could pray for her, Catherine's response seemed strange.

"Can you pray that I toughen up a little bit? I cannot be crying all the time when these kids die."

She went on to explain that Malawians are very stoic and it was unsettling for a mother when the weird white doctor who was doing weird things to her baby was crying and looking guilty. She felt that her out-of-control emotions were making the situation worse.

"I don't want to *not* care. I just want a guitar callus."

When you first start playing the guitar, she explained, the tips of your fingers feel like they've been sunburned or burned on a hot pot. They're tender, red, and painful. But as you persevere, you build up calluses, and you can play the music without as much pain.

"What I want is to be able to show up every day and play the music without falling apart. I want to be able to be a witness to these women when their children pass away. I want to toughen up enough to still do my job and be a testimony."

The losses are still there, the circumstances are still difficult, but with resources in place now to help her process it all, she is able to hold a perspective on the situation with peace.

Over the years, Catherine has helped a lot of desperate mothers and their babies. Sadly, in Malawi, they see a lot of pit latrine babies. Mothers in desperate situations—threatened to be murdered or have their house destroyed if they became pregnant—hide the pregnancy and then, unthinkably, discard the baby in the pit latrine. Yes, it really is unfathomable. . . but also understandable when you know the intense social situations they're living in.

Women have very few rights in Malawi. They and their children belong to their husbands. For this reason, it's very hard for a woman to leave a domestic violence situation. She won't be protected by the police if she runs away. And if she does run away, she'll have to leave her children behind. These painful village dynamics combined with extreme poverty lead mothers to make choices that, under other circumstances, would be unthinkable.

These are Catherine's patients. These are the circumstances where Catherine serves.

HOPE FOR THE BABIES

After a rest in the United States and giving birth to her second child, Catherine returned to Malawi to a new request. Would she consider starting a new unit in the hospital to care for very sick babies? It seemed God was going to put those calluses to the test.

At that time no neonatal care was offered in Malawi. Practically speaking, that meant if a baby was sick, had a fever, or wasn't breastfeeding, they just lay in bed next to their mother and passed away. This was not just at Nkhoma Hospital but all over the country. There were no country guidelines on neonatal care and no neonatal medical equipment.

For neonatal care in a hospital setting, you need a few basic things. You need phototherapy lamps, and you need warmers. Even in the sub-Saharan African warm season, tiny infants die of hypothermia because they simply don't have enough fat to regulate their body temperature. You also need equipment that allows for tiny amounts of IV fluids and pressurized oxygen support. Regular oxygen through the nose will not help premature babies stay alive. They need to have extra pressure because their lungs are too immature to keep themselves open.

It's a fine line between life and death, and the victims are the least of these.

Flexibility and slowly growing guitar callus perspective working in tandem, Catherine accepted the challenge. In her family medicine training, she'd only had two weeks of neonatal rotation, but she dove into the task of educating herself. Slow internet speeds at the compound didn't allow her to take advantage of online resources, and even email was cumbersome, so she went old school, poring over textbooks and anything else she could get her hands on.

With the help of a couple of pediatricians from Ireland, over the next six months, the doctors wrote all the protocols for treating these tiny, sick babies. And over the next year, they built a neonatal unit from scratch, starting with an empty room with a tile floor.

To flexibility, they added ingenuity. As they researched equipment, if they didn't find anything that fit the bill, they designed it themselves.

One of those things was hot cots. Made from plywood, they are small boxes with warming lights underneath and a little space so the hot air can rise and go up over the baby. Four light bulbs create enough heat to keep a tiny baby warm. Since starting to use these, they've not had a single hypothermic death. And because flexibility is the name of the game, they are now switching to chicken coop lights. Regular light bulbs have been discontinued in Malawi for environmental reasons, and chicken lights are the only hot lights allowed in the country.

Prior to opening the neonatal unit, there was high infant mortality, and seemingly, the hospital staff wasn't invested in changing that. All that changed when they moved to their own unit. With the newly outfitted unit up and running, the infant care team moved out of the maternity unit and gained dedicated neonatal staff. Now the nurses could focus solely on taking care of the infants, rather than being asked to take care of both the mothers and the very sick babies. With only one patient to care for and the proper equipment, there was hope for the babies at last. These Malawian nurses, who had seen so much death and hopeless situations in their careers, had new passion and spark.

Within the first few months of opening the ward, Catherine had an experience with a Malawian mother and her twin babies that changed her perspective again. When it came time to discharge the mother and the babies from the hospital, Catherine was filling out the required paperwork, including the babies' names. Often Malawian mothers will not name the baby immediately but will take a few days to consult with the father or the grand-mother. But by the time they discharge, they have usually settled on a name.

Speaking in Chichewa, the mother told Catherine the babies' names were *Mavuto* and *Chisoni*. Catherine, not able to speak Chichewa and having no idea what these names meant, repeated the babies' names to make sure she understood the pronunciation and was writing them down correctly.

"Mavuto and Chisoni? Is that correct?"

A rumble of booing came from the other mothers in the ward. The mother looked down, embarrassed, but she wasn't giggling. She was resolved.

"Those are their names."

Malawian mothers often name their babies based on their experiences or how they feel about that child. Sometimes the name is offered as a future blessing over their child. Names like Grace, Scholastica, Divine, or Precious are not uncommon. Understanding this cultural practice, Catherine knew she had to get to the bottom of this. She quickly tracked down a female chaplain assigned to the maternity and neonatal units and asked what the names meant. Why would the other mothers be so bothered by these names?

Because they meant *Trouble* and *Sorrow*.

The chaplain learned that this woman's husband had infected her with HIV and then abandoned her when she became pregnant. She was going home to a completely desperate situation. The hopelessness was too much. She could not say a blessing over her babies. She couldn't see blessing as a possibility. She saw only trouble and sorrow ahead.

But the rest of the story proves that God can work blessings even in the most heartbreaking circumstances. After speaking with the chaplain that day and learning about the hope found only in Christ, this mother became a Christian. And before she left the hospital, she had a request for Dr. Catherine. She asked if she could change her babies' names.

"Zikomo and Yamikani. These are their new names."

Thanks and *Praise*. Two simple words, filled with so much hope.

As Catherine shared this story with me, she couldn't help but tear up, saying, "That day, that experience, changed something in my DNA."

The hope of Christ entered into a hopeless heart that day. This is the core of what it means to be a medical missionary—physical and spiritual healing.

HOPE IN CHRIST

Together, Catherine and Dave work to offer hope in Christ. In the hospital, that looks like working with the chaplains to provide care and encouragement to patients like Thanks and Praise's mom. Or it can look like discipling residents in training as Catherine teaches them the nuances of tropical medicine. Along with a fellow doctor, she leads a weekly Bible study for residents and offers an annual spiritual retreat for staff and their spouses.

Dave works with Young Life, a Bible study group for high school students. He trains leaders and leads his own group. He also does a hermeneutical Bible study with villagers who are literate in their own language of Chichewa or in English, which is the business language of Malawi. Though Dave doesn't speak Chichewa, he can still help local pastors as they minister in their village churches.

At the hospital or in the community, they're living out their calling.

INSIGHT, WISDOM, AND TAKEAWAYS

Catherine recalls a dark time about two years after their arrival in Malawi. In addition to the day-to-day struggles, they had a string of close calls with venomous snakes and their children. She found herself losing her joy, experiencing dark thoughts, and then, finally, awakening in the middle of the night with panic attacks.

At that point Dave encouraged her to seek out help from their sending organization. They connected her with the appropriate resources, and it was instantly helpful. So her advice? Seek help early and often. Don't wait for a crisis. She and Dave still get regular therapy, though it's less frequent now.

Another piece of advice was shared by a veteran missionary. He cautioned Catherine and Dave not to look back at the end of the first year to assess your accomplishments. You will wonder why you left your family and electricity and other comforts, and you will feel pretty bad about it one year in, he said. Don't look back until you've been there at least five years. Because it's only over time that you can see the sweet fruit of God's work in and around you.

Also, learn to acknowledge the hard. Many years ago, Catherine read a sentence that has stuck with her, "Pity weeps and walks away, but compassion stays to suffer." As a medical missionary, you will see and possibly experience unspeakable suffering. As a Christian and a doctor, you must learn how to grieve and lament in a healthy way. Like Peter in John 6, turn to Jesus in moments of weariness and say, "Where else will I go? You hold the words of life."

This *perspective* describes Catherine's philosophy, and her work is bearing much fruit.

CHAPTER 6

JOHN CROPSEY

SIGHT

As a little boy in Togo, West Africa, John Cropsey was no stranger to the mission hospital—not because he was prone to injury or was a sickly child, but because his dad, Bob, was the doctor.

But let's back up a bit, because John's childhood on the mission field is directly connected to Bob's childhood in rural Michigan and an old-time tent revival. A visiting missionary and Bible translator from Africa told a story of his time in a small African village—the kind of story that any twelve-year-old boy would lean in to hear.

As the missionary told it, the villagers were resistant to the gospel, refusing to engage with the message. One day something happened to change all that. A child from the village had been injured. He'd somehow had an accident, and it didn't look good. A busted open gut and protruding bowels were just part of the problem.

At this point, I'm sure all the boys in the room couldn't wait to hear more gory details.

Although the missionary wasn't a medical missionary, he did have a first aid kit and a can-do spirit. So using boiling water, antibiotic powder, and horsehair for thread—and praying for a miracle—this missionary was able to get those slippery bowels back in the boy and sew him up. Somehow the boy didn't die.

For John's dad, this story changed the trajectory of his life. He wanted to be a missionary. Like the man who told the story in that revival tent in the middle of a Michigan cornfield, young Bob wanted to serve as the hands and feet of Jesus in Africa. And he wanted to do it as a *doctor*.

So that's what he did. He studied hard in high school, ignoring the comments of a counselor who questioned if he was doctor material. He went to college, married his high school sweetheart, and finished medical school. He started making a plan to get to Africa.

And when John Cropsey was four years old, his dad—now Dr. Bob Cropsey—moved his wife (a nurse) and their four boys to Togo.

Dr. Cropsey, along with another general surgeon, went to start a hospital from scratch, carving it out of the jungle and building it up over the years. John loved growing up at the mission hospital. Seeing the impact of what his parents were doing on people's lives both physically and spiritually was very inspiring.

When it came time for John to pick a course of study after high school, medicine and medical missions were the natural choices.

He assumed he would follow in his father's footsteps and become a general surgeon, but he also recalled how tied to the hospital his father had been. Because the needs were so great and his father was often the only doctor of any kind available, he did general surgery. But he also did obstetrics and gynecology, neurosurgery, pediatrics, ophthalmology—anything that was needed.

So John started asking questions. He asked his dad and a few other jungle surgeons, "If you could do it over again, what type of medicine would you practice?"

Overwhelmingly, the replies came back, "I would be an ophthalmologist."

Interesting.

John's dad recounted that one of the most moving experiences he'd had as a doctor was performing a cataract surgery on a patient that allowed him to see his grandchild for the first time. To perform a ten minute surgery that took people from blindness to sight within hours was simply amazing. Ophthalmology residents John spoke with agreed. They all loved their jobs. Feeling like he'd stumbled upon the best-kept secret in medicine, John went full speed ahead toward the goal of becoming an ophthalmologist.

During his medical training, John and his wife, Jessica, became friends with two other couples in their church who were also in residency. Among the three couples, there were four doctors—each with a different specialty. Providentially, they all finished their residency training at the same time, and *all* had a desire to serve God as missionaries.

After a period of planning, they did something amazing: they moved to Kenya as a team. But that was just the beginning. After serving together there for two years, God refined their vision for the future. When many people think of missions, they often think of relief efforts or church planting and evangelism. John and his friends had a different aim in mind.

They wanted to be a team focused primarily on medical education. As much as they loved their time with patients, they realized that multiplication was a better strategy, and the way to do that was to train people in-country. If they really wanted to make a difference, they were convinced that they needed to multiply themselves exponentially by developing local capacity. If they were really going to bring healthcare on a meaningful scale to places without access, they wanted to sink their careers into training African doctors.

As they started looking at countries in Africa where they might be able to pursue this mission, they realized a certain level of political stability would be required. This ruled out any active war zone countries.

After much prayer, research, and conversation, they ended up partnering with Hope Africa University, a Christian university in Burundi that was working to develop a teaching hospital, Kibuye Hope Hospital.

Just like before, they made the move as a team.

Burundi is one of the poorest nations in the world. The country endured over a decade of war, impacted by the challenges in Rwanda and Congo. The conditions on the ground were challenging, and the need was astronomical. At the time there were only approximately 300 doctors in the entire country—a country of over 12 million people.

When John and his team did a site visit to Hope Africa University in 2010, the medical school faculty consisted of one residency-trained Burundian doctor (an OB-GYN) and three general medical officers from Congo. It was a perfect place for their team to land.

When they moved to Burundi in 2013, they had six specialists in six different fields. From their original team, they had an ophthalmologist, general surgeon, OB-GYN, and a family practitioner.

They had added two more doctors who shared the vision—a pediatrician (med-peds) and an ER doctor. It was a robust team with a focused goal.

When they arrived, the facilities of Kibuye Hope Hospital were in rough shape. There was barely running water. All the buildings needed to be gutted and have new electrical systems installed. An old ward turned storage room was transformed into an eye clinic.

Eight years later, what God helped them build was amazing: a three-hundred-plus-bed teaching hospital.

Hope Africa University and Kibuye Hope Hospital have trained more than an additional three hundred (at the time of this writing) doctors, and they are still going strong. As impressive as that is, John knows it's not just about treating the eyes of his fellow man.

It's also about the heart of God.

I love the way he said it: "Medical missions *is* the kingdom of God. In the gospel of Luke, Jesus said, 'I've come to set the prisoner free, to heal the blind, to help the lame walk.' That's the gospel too. It's all part of the same thing: God's kingdom coming in word *and deed*."

The gift of sight.

As John began acclimating to practicing medicine in Burundi, he continued to be amazed at the immediate impact specialized eye care could have on people's health and quality of life. Working in the hospital and on outreach trips, he saw firsthand again and again how simple medical care could make a major difference. On a trip partnering with Samaritan's Purse in South Sudan, he and a Kenyan physician assistant performed over five hundred cataract surgeries during the course of six days. Those five hundred blind eyes that could then see were five hundred lives impacted by both the physical and spiritual healing of the gospel.

FROM RELIEF TO DEVELOPMENT

From cataract surgeries to comprehensive care, John loves treating patients, but for as much joy as that brings him, he's firmly focused on teaching and education as his first priority. He and his team like to say, "We're not the best people for this job. Our students are!"

Doctors in his father's generation labored for years, impacting their communities and making a difference in thousands of lives, but also laying a foundation for the development work that John's generation aims to tackle. John says he could treat patients day and night his whole career, and it would be a drop in the bucket. To really make a difference, he wants to multiply himself by training local people.

As he treats patients, he's also training future medical professionals. He's building the local ability to do the work. The three hundred new doctors they've trained know the local language and culture, and they understand where the patients are coming from in a much deeper way than foreigners are able to. It's a powerful blend of vision and execution.

As John teaches the medical details, he is also discipling. Together he and his residents explore what it means to practice medicine when you're not just a doctor but a Christian doctor compelled by the love of Christ.

It's a big goal, but John and his wife, Jessica, feel that God has given them a vision to tackle blindness in Africa. Today eight out of ten blind people in Africa are blind from preventable or treatable causes. They simply don't have access to the care they need. That's why John and Jessica recently made the difficult decision to leave Burundi and their team there and join an African couple starting an ophthalmology residency program at an eye institute in Rwanda. Their new focus is entirely on eye care. They are currently training and discipling eye surgeons from Rwanda, Congo, Burundi, and Kenya.

John's desire is to create the best eye training center in Africa, if not the world.

SENDING THE TRAINED

John's goal is to build up his African brothers and sisters as medical professionals and missionaries and see where God takes them to provide physical and spiritual healing.

Dr. Toney is one of those medical professionals.

A Burundian, Dr. Toney was born at Kibuye and went on to graduate from Hope Africa University's medical school. He then joined John and worked alongside him to start the eye clinic. After about a year of working together, John encouraged him to continue his education to become an ophthalmologist, which at that time required leaving the country. Three years later, he came back to rejoin John as a trained ophthalmologist. In addition to working in the clinic, together they made several outreach trips to Congo. Dr. Toney was so inspired and convicted by the huge needs he saw in Congo that he ended up moving there.

Part of the beauty of this model of missions as development is that trained local doctors can take medicine and the gospel into places American doctors like John could never reach. In Dr. Toney's case, that meant deep inside Congo, to a huge province the size of England that has never had an ophthalmologist.

This is Dr. Toney's clinic. The jungle is his operating room.

In an effort to connect Western hearts to African need, John's mission organization, Serge, partnered with Dr. Toney to help get him set up in Congo. They also sponsor him to do six outreaches a year to remote territories where there is no eye care. The roads to these areas—if they even exist—are impassible most of the year. The team flies on a small charter plane owned by other NGOs to whatever airstrip is nearest to their final destination. They then sometimes have to take motorcycles for another four hours, carrying surgical microscopes and other equipment on their laps or lashed to the back of their motorcycles.

Dr. Toney is able to have a profound impact in these remote places. Amazingly, this partnership allowed Dr. Toney to perform *one thousand cataract surgeries* in his first year in Congo, bringing sight to the blind and spreading the light of Christ.

Dr. Alliance is another powerful story. He was in the very first graduating class of Hope Africa University's medical school. Here's how John relates the story:

> MedSend contacted our team while we were studying French in Albertville, France, in preparation for teaching in Burundi. They asked us if we knew of someone they could sponsor as their pilot national scholar. Dr. Alliance immediately came to mind. He was exceptional and had a huge heart to serve Christ through medicine. He wanted to be a surgeon. With MedSend's help, he was sponsored to do a surgical residency at Bongolo Mission Hospital in Gabon.

It wasn't all easy. Alliance and his wife, Cynthia, had many challenges, including losing a child. But they persisted. Dr. Alliance finished his surgical training and joined John's team at Kibuye. For John, it was a dream come true. This was proof of the multiplication principle they hoped to build when they first moved to Kenya and began their ministry—the trainee now becoming the teacher of the next generation of African healthcare providers.

Cynthia also got involved in using her gift. She joined the retinoblastoma team as its program manager. Again, it's best to hear the story in John's own words:

She was amazing. One day I came into the chemo ward to see her and another retinoblastoma teammate with a cake, candles, and balloons to celebrate a little girl's birthday. This little girl had come too late and had to have both of her eyes removed in order to try to save her life. Cynthia brought a smile to this family's faces that day. I will never forget how Cynthia and her colleagues loved those kids with retinoblastoma.

Their work isn't done. Dr. Alliance has since gone on to do a fellowship in pediatric surgery in Malawi. He is nearly finished, and only God knows how He'll use Alliance and Cynthia in the coming years.

This is the heartbeat of medical missions.

PUSHING THROUGH THE PAIN

Word about John's hospital and eye clinic and eye surgeries that can cure blindness spread. After some of those outreach trips to Congo, people began traveling to Burundi seeking help and hoping for sight.

One day a man and his twenty-three-year-old son arrived at the clinic to see John. The man had been blind for twenty-six years and had never seen his son's face. They had traveled three days to reach the clinic. John was afraid the man had some irreversible problem, but upon examining him, John discovered he simply had cataracts. He'd been blind *for twenty-six years* from a reversible condition. They performed the surgery, and the next day this man was able to see his adult son and his grandson for the first time.

This is the kind of joyful result that encourages missionary doctors to stay the course. Bringing sight to the blind is one of the highlights of providing eye care in Africa.

Other parts of the job can be devastatingly heartbreaking. There are difficult days that cause even seasoned missionaries like John to question the goodness of God.

Many Burundians experience bone-crushing poverty and unspeakable suffering. John recalls when, during an especially difficult period of personal struggle, an infant was brought to his clinic. For reasons unknown, but not unheard of, the child's mother had discarded the baby in a pit latrine. Someone had rescued the baby, but not before he had experienced chemical burns on his eyes that would leave them scarred shut, rendering him blind for the rest of his life.

Into the horrible situation came a Burundian nun. As a follower of Jesus, she was prepared to take this baby as her own and raise him. She was prepared to love and care for a child someone else had discarded. Her incarnational love touched his heart.

This is just one story.

One of the most difficult things John faces as an ophthalmologist is children with retinoblastoma—a type of disfiguring, painful, socially ostracizing eye cancer. Without treatment, it is nearly one hundred percent fatal. And until recently, there'd been no chemotherapy treatment available for any kind of cancer in Burundi. Even if families could somehow afford to leave the country, most sought treatment only when it was too late for chemo to be effective.

Year after year as John saw all these kids coming in facing continued suffering and inevitable death, he decided he had to do something about it. Convincing his pediatrician colleague and several Burundian nurses to join him, they all traveled to Rwanda to get trained on how to administer chemotherapy for retinoblastoma. Then they started the first chemo program in the country of Burundi. Since 2020, they've been able to treat over 120 kids with retinoblastoma, saving lives and returning dignity to suffering families.

John doesn't have an answer for the problem of evil or pain. Living in the poverty of Burundi or in the shadow of Rwandan genocide, he finds no answer other than Jesus. Jesus entered into human pain with us. This is what makes our God different. Our God came near to us. Our God came to suffer with us. And it's this truth that keeps John going.

Our God cares enough to get His hands dirty with us. And someday everything will be made right. In the meantime, John and his African colleagues are doing all they can to alleviate that suffering and to share the hope that is found in Christ.

INSIGHT, WISDOM, AND TAKEAWAYS

As an undergrad thinking about being a medical missionary, John asked a veteran jungle surgeon for his best advice. In addition to recommending ophthalmology, he urged John to *learn humility*.

John agrees with the quip that says being a missionary is like sprinkling MiracleGro on your sin. The many stressors and challenges that come with missionary life expose your weaknesses and faults and magnify your problems.

But that's actually a gift.

It's from that place of weakness that you can truly minister. Humility, brokenness, and the gospel at work in those places in our lives is actually what we want to show the world. It's not our strength and how wonderful we are, but how broken and needy we are and how Jesus enters into that. It's only with an identity firmly rooted in Christ that we are able to stand. You are a child of God, and nothing else really matters. If your mission efforts succeed or fail, that's in God's hands. Our identity is not wrapped up in that.

It's wrapped up in who we are in Christ. And that's more than enough.

CHAPTER 7

BOAZ NIYINYUMVA

LISTEN AND GO

The Niyinyumva family faced an impossible choice. Two years earlier, civil war in their home country of Burundi had forced them to flee to the Democratic Republic of the Congo (DRC). Now the same chaos from which they had fled had come to DRC, and they found themselves twice displaced—double refugees. What could they do? Where should they go? Their options were grim: make a harrowing overland journey to Tanzania where they would continue to be refugees, or return to Burundi.

They chose Burundi, thinking if they were going to die, they wanted to die in their own country.

But that led to another impossible choice. How to get home? Again, there were only two options, and neither was good. Lake Tanganyika runs along the border of Burundi and the DRC, but the Burundian military had closed the lake to travel. Anyone caught crossing was considered a rebel and killed on the spot.

To travel by road wasn't much better; it meant passing through military checkpoints of the invading army. And they had heard the rumors. Everyone was being stopped, and all the men and boys were being killed.

If they stayed in the DRC, they would die no matter what. To go by canoe across Lake Tanganyika was risky, but at least there was a fifty-fifty chance. Maybe they would be caught, and maybe they wouldn't. Traveling by road meant almost certain death for the men and boys.

So they made the impossible decision to split the family up. Eleven-year-old Boaz and his father and brother would take their chances by water, and his mother and sisters would travel by road.

On the day his mother and sisters left, Boaz stayed home while his father and brother went to scout out the options for getting a canoe that evening to take them across the lake. Four hours after they had left, Boaz heard a voice speaking.

"Boaz, stand up and follow your mother."

Without question or hesitation, he packed a small bag and set out. There was only one road they could have taken, so he was not concerned about getting lost or taking the wrong way. With his bag slung over his shoulder, he began walking, asking someone every once in a while, "Have you seen a group of Burundian women pass this way?"

Occasionally, someone with a bicycle would offer him a ride.

As he made his way, unbeknownst to him, he managed to get ahead of his mother and sisters. They had taken a detour in the city to join up with some other women, figuring they'd be safer in a larger group. If an entire group was killed, it would create an international scandal, while a single woman and her daughters would be of no consequence.

After a full day of walking and hitching rides and not seeing his mother and sisters, Boaz was tired, dusty, and hungry. He stopped near a sugarcane market and lay down under a mango tree to rest. The next thing he knew, he heard a voice calling, "Is that Boaz?"

His mother and the other women had stopped at the sugarcane market to buy food and happened to see him sleeping under the mango tree.

Amazed and overjoyed to be united, they also knew the risk of traveling with a boy. But Boaz was small and thin, and with a slight change of clothes, he was easily disguised as a young girl. In this way they passed the checkpoints, and no one gave them any trouble.

Back in Burundi, as they began to rebuild some sort of a life, they learned the sad news: Boaz's father and brother had taken their chances on the water and did not make it. They were killed by the military.

Boaz was the only one left to carry on the Niyinyumva name.

THE CALLING

Like many young boys around the world who have dreams of flying, Boaz dreamed of being a military pilot. But life circumstances have a way of altering dreams. In the refugee camp in the DRC, his sensitive heart was burdened by the suffering around him. He saw the lack of food and basic medical care. He recalls playing with other children one day and then never seeing them again because they had died in the night—often from diarrhea or malaria or some other preventable disease.

Boaz was angry, sad, and confused. This should not be happening. Even in his young heart, he had an inkling: *Why have I survived when so many others have not? If I had some skill, I could help these children.*

It was in the harsh environment of the refugee camp back in the DRC that God first spoke to Boaz. He had grown up with a solid background in Christian education. He knew about God speaking to Samuel and David and others in the Bible. So when he heard a voice talking to him in his brain, calling him, he listened.

In his anger and sorrow, he heard God say, *Boaz, you will be a doctor. Someday you will help people like this.*

But soon after that came the dramatic trip out of the DRC and the sad news about his father and brother.

Back in Burundi, Boaz, as the oldest male, became the breadwinner for the family at age eleven. The voice of God and the calling in the refugee camp were far from his mind. Life went on. And the life that went on was hard. It was a struggle simply to find food for the family.

One day a friend of his father's came to the house.

"Your father and I made a pact," he said, "that if either of us died, we would take care of the other's children. I have many children. I cannot take all of you to school, but I will take two of you, Boaz, you and your sister."

Going to school was a wonderful change, but life continued to be hard. Boaz remembers going for days in a row with no food—not even a little breakfast. But somehow he found himself still succeeding in school. He may have been hungry, but he was sharp. He was small in size but competed academically with those much older and bigger. With the help of his father's friend and other people God brought into his life, he made it to high school.

He did not take a science track; instead his studies focused more on the arts. He did a bit of mathematics, chemistry and biology, but the emphasis was on literature and history. Even so, somehow he was good at math and science, and he was able to compete with those in the science track.

When it came time to sit for university entrance exams, Boaz was one of 150 students who took the exam. It covered everything—arts, economics, science, math. And out of all the students, amazingly (but perhaps not surprisingly), Boaz got the second-highest marks.

EDUCATION

Those high scores earned him the right to apply for a university and indicate his top three choices for a major area of study. A committee would then consider his choices and his performance and match him with a course of study accordingly.

At this point, though he was a believer, Boaz was not understanding the work of God in his life. So much time had passed since those years in the refugee camp; so much life had happened. He was simply continuing with the next step in his life, and as he looked at the form to indicate his choices, the call of God was not on his mind.

Rather, his first choice, law, was guided by revenge. He wanted revenge against the people who had killed his father and brother. His second choice, medicine, was chosen for acclaim. Medicine was a noble profession. And his third choice? Again, law. If he selected law twice, surely, he thought, the committee would see that was the best choice.

But their decision? Medicine.

And that's when it clicked. Boaz sat back and started remembering. He remembered God's call in the refugee camp, the people God brought into his life, and how God had directed him each step of the way.

Okay, God, I see it. I accept it. I am going. I will study medicine.

But again, there was the question of money.

Without financial support, private medical school was not an option. Though public school wasn't ideal, there didn't seem to be another choice. To attend the public school, he would be required to wait one year before beginning, and even then the public school was full of scandal and drama. One year of studies could drag out to as many as three calendar years because of strikes and other disruptions. Not ideal, but Boaz was committed. If this was God's plan, he would do it.

During the year of waiting, he joined a Korean missionary to travel the country providing vacation Bible school classes for children. If he had to wait a year, he might as well do something significant.

When the time came to start medical school, his first "year" of studies took twenty months to complete due to teacher and student strikes. This was not a sustainable way to achieve an education.

God, this cannot happen. If it is You who brought me to this, I want to go to a private university so that I can study and finish. I don't know how You are going to do that, but I believe that You can.

And in a bold step of faith, Boaz registered for classes at a private Christian medical school while still completing exams at the national university.

One day his Korean missionary friend asked how the studies were going.

"They're not," Boaz said. And then he explained all that was happening and that he wanted to go to a private university somehow.

"Which university do you want to attend? Go. Register there, and I will pay for it."

And again, it clicked for Boaz. That one-year delay was not a waste of time. It allowed him to build a relationship with this man and for him to see that God had plans for his life. When it came time for that Korean missionary to return home, and he could no longer support Boaz, God provided another benefactor to help Boaz finish his education. In fact, when he finished, there was enough money in his school account to pay for someone else.

A MATTER OF THE HEART

At the end of medical school in Burundi, Boaz completed an internship in a rural village outside the city. This was a place where poverty was impossible to ignore. You could see it; you could smell it.

Boaz was no stranger to poverty. He remembered what it was like to go without food, to wonder every day if there would be enough. He knew what it was like to feel as if your family was only one small incident away from disaster. He understood why people stayed at home suffering, simply waiting for a miracle, because there were no funds for medical care. He felt an immediate bond with these patients. He could see himself in them.

And in serving these poor people in this rural village, his calling became even more clear: *These are the people you should serve. This is where you belong.*

Throughout medical school, Boaz had been focused on the heart. Cardiology was his interest and passion. He had accepted God's call to be a doctor. And after this internship experience, he had accepted the call to work among the poor. Yet he really wanted to be a cardiologist. He loved everything related to the heart. But who among the poor can afford a cardiologist? In a setting where people cannot even pay for a single tablet of Tylenol, what could a cardiologist offer?

Again, the hand of God moved in an unexpected way.

When Boaz applied to a government hospital for his first job after medical school, the hospital asked for a bribe equivalent to five months' salary—a bribe for the privilege of having a job. Despite the financial implications, Boaz refused. He was not interested in getting involved in this type of corruption. He had not come this far for God to not continue to provide a way. So he stayed home. He did not work for three months. But during those uncertain months, God was working His plan.

At that time a missionary doctor who had taught at Boaz's medical school organized a three-month outreach trip to the DRC. Boaz had no intention of joining him. Why go back there? Why Congo? But days before the trip, the medical student who planned to go backed out and volunteered Boaz. He wasn't working. He didn't have a good excuse to refuse. So he agreed. He went back to the place where his medical calling had begun.

This time it was not a refugee camp but a village. But just like before, people were suffering, and children were dying. Boaz began treating patients—young children, pregnant women, men— anyone who had need. He acted as a surgeon, gynecologist, pediatrician, and internist. And one thought reverberated through his mind: *God, I'm not equipped to do this. I don't have the knowledge.*

In those three months, his desire to become a cardiologist was replaced by an overwhelming desire for broad knowledge across all ages and diseases. He wanted to become everything for everybody. How could he accomplish that? What would that look like? Cardiology was not the answer, but what was the alternative?

And again, God brought someone into his life. The day after he arrived back in Burundi, he met someone who connected him to a doctor in Kenya. It turned out that this doctor wanted to start a family medicine residency training program. As he explained to Boaz what the program included, his description met perfectly what Boaz had been praying for. Boaz started making plans to go to Kenya to study family medicine at Kabarak Mission Hospital.

But what about the school fees?

Enter the MedSend National Scholars program.

The National Scholars Program sponsors advanced medical training for Christian national physicians—training that many would not be able to afford on their own. MedSend partners with established in-country, Christ-centered medical residency programs like the one Boaz was headed to in Kenya. These residency programs not only provide advanced medical training but also spiritual development and leadership preparation.

Thanks to the financial assistance from MedSend and another benefactor, Boaz was able to complete the advanced training to become a family medicine physician, something he never would have imagined possible.

MULTIPLICATION

After completing family practice residency, Boaz took a position as the family medicine program coordinator at a mission hospital in rural Kenya, the position he still holds today. As program coordinator, not only does he treat patients, but he also provides training and education for medical students, physician assistants, nurses, and general healthcare workers. He's committed to multiplying what he's received—training the next generation of healthcare leaders who share the love of God through the compassionate care they provide. He has a vision for healthcare workers to treat patients not as illnesses or diseases only but as precious children of God who need care and compassion.

He and his wife, along with his two children, are national missionaries, supported by a mission organization. In addition to the hospital work, they are involved in community development and helping children attain an education through school.

At the time of this writing, as Boaz is joyfully serving in Kenya, his sights are still set on home. He and several others are actively trying to build a family medicine training program in Burundi. Boaz was the first Burundian to be trained in family medicine, and there are now several others. Boaz wants to go home to Burundi to serve his people, and he wants to continue to multiply himself. The need for qualified, compassionate care is great, and he wants to expand the impact he can have by training other Burundians as family physicians.

The government-required paperwork is in process. Boaz and his small team have met with the Burundian authorities in the Ministry of Health and Ministry of Education. They have designed a curriculum. And now they are waiting for the curriculum to be approved and for direction for the next steps in the process.

They hope not only to change healthcare in Burundi but also to impact people spiritually. Through the fruits of the Holy Spirit on display as they train and treat, they hope to reach one family each year and disciple them into followers of Jesus.

Africa has seen multiple revivals, but they haven't always resulted in true followers. Boaz and his team aren't interested in simply expanding the number of Christians. Through words and actions and the powerful movement of the Holy Spirit, they are looking forward to seeing lives truly changed and true disciples made.

As he looks back on those internship days when his overwhelming thought was that he was not equipped to meet the needs he saw, he sees those years of education and practical experience in Kenya have given him confidence.

"I am medically equipped, socially equipped, spiritually equipped, so I can't wait until God tells me, 'Okay, now it's time. Are you ready to go back to Burundi?'"

INSIGHT, WISDOM, AND TAKEAWAYS

What a journey it has been. From calling him as a child in a refugee camp, saving him from death, and guiding him through times of sorrow and lack and uncertainty, Boaz sees how God has provided a way for him over and over again. At every stage of his life, God brought people to help him be what God wanted him to be.

Without a doubt, Boaz's greatest joy is serving people. Is that due to personality? Perhaps. But it also flows from a profound sense of having been loved himself.

"I got more than I deserved," he says. "Why did I survive when my brother and so many others did not? Why did so many people help me get where I am today? It's all linked to the love of Jesus. I am nothing other than a product of the love of God, and I want to share that with others who are in need. "

CHAPTER 8

BELYSE ARAKAZA

CONFUSE THE SCIENCE

D r. Belyse Arakaza is a Christian doctor. Not a doctor who happens to be a Christian. That's very clear to her. And it makes all the difference.

As a young girl growing up in Burundi, East Africa, Belyse first entertained the idea of being a doctor when a high school biology course captured her attention. And then one year during the holidays, one of Belyse's relatives became ill and was admitted to the hospital. While there visiting her, the sick family member collapsed on Belyse, and she panicked. But even in her panic, she managed to put her cousin back into bed and get her settled. That simple experience felt to Belyse like a doctor's kind of act—like doctors are heroes and really can make a difference.

So when toward the end of high school, her uncle, who was helping manage her academics, took a look at her grades and announced, "You should do medicine," it was easy for Belyse to agree. She had caught the vision of how a doctor could impact others' lives, and she wanted to be a part of that. Medicine it was.

With hard work and determination, she threw herself into medical school. During an internship at a mission hospital clinic, she met a family physician missionary who had a profound effect on her life. She saw the way he treated patients with patience and kindness. She saw him praying with the patients. She experienced him and other instructors taking time for devotions and Bible study and discussing questions of faith with the large class of interns.

Watching this family physician, Belyse thought, *This is the kind of person I want to become when I grow up. This is the kind of doctor I want to be.*

Belyse wasn't interested in being a doctor Monday through Saturday and then a Christian only on Sunday. She felt like there had to be a way of integrating the two, and watching this doctor, she got a picture of what that could look like and was inspired.

When it came time to choose a specialty after medical school, family medicine appealed to Belyse because a family doctor can be everything to everyone. A family doctor can deliver a baby, can be a pediatrician to a child, can treat hypertension and diabetes and malaria—a bit of everything. She admits she may be biased, but she believes family medicine is the best specialty for Africa right now because there is such a shortage of other specialists, such as obstetricians or pediatricians. A family physician can step into that gap and meet people at their point of need.

The only catch was that there was no way to train in family medicine in Burundi, so she had to go to Kenya to Kabarak University. This is where MedSend came in.

Medical school is expensive no matter where you are in the world. Africa is no exception. By this time, Belyse was married and had a child. A scholarship from the MedSend National Scholars Program paid for part of her tuition and living expenses for the four years of specialty training. MedSend was the key to her being able to complete this training; it simply wouldn't have been possible without that financial assistance. Her parents died when she was young, so going through medical school and residency was, in her words, a pure miracle.

And beyond the practical financial help, to Belyse, that support felt like a message from God—a message that He cares and that He truly is a Father to the fatherless.

REFOCUS AND REDEFINE

Determined to make the most of this generous provision, Belyse engaged her studies with all she had. But in the middle of it, she got tired. Juggling studies and long hours at the hospital and caring for her family became too much, and she simply burned out.

The final straw came when her tiny son's first spoken word was the name of his nanny, not hers. It was more than she could take.

I'm failing here. I am failing there. This is bad.

The fatigue and the expectations from the training were overwhelming. She wanted to quit. She almost walked out, but she decided to visit the hospital chaplain first. Her intention was to say goodbye and explain the reasons for her leaving.

He patiently listened as she poured out how tired, discouraged, and helpless she felt. And then he simply said, "Rebuild your relationship with the Lord."

She was taken aback and at first a little defensive. What was he saying? What was he accusing her of?

But in her heart, she knew he was right. She had stopped her devotions—her Bible reading and prayer. Not without good reason. After all, her time was severely limited. Early mornings and exhausting days meant she was barely hanging on. But this lack of regular spiritual food was killing her.

She knew she had lost sight of the bigger picture. She was focusing on performance, doing everything right, being a good resident, being a good doctor. She was determined to refocus. She asked herself some questions:

At the end of all this, is God being glorified?
Yes, I treated this patient's hypertension, but what if he dies today? Did I share the good news with him?
What am I doing that has eternal value?

The next day she woke up fifteen minutes earlier than usual and opened her Bible for the first time in a long time. She read the scripture from Matthew 11:28–30 that says:

Come to me, all who labor and are heavy laden, and I will give you rest. Take my yoke upon you, and learn from me, for I am gentle and lowly in heart, and you will find rest for your souls. For my yoke is easy, and my burden is light.

As she rebuilt her relationship with God, the responsibility of performing was not removed. She still wanted to be the best doctor she could be and give her patients the best care possible. But it was no longer her primary focus. Living as a Christian *first* and doctor *second* removed the pressure and opened her eyes to new opportunities.

Medicine became the vehicle to show Christ and share the good news.

Renewed, she soon passed her exams and became a full-time family physician at Kijabe Hospital in Kenya.

Today her days continue to be full, but in the best possible way. They are a mix of patient care (adult, pediatric outpatient, or emergency), resident and intern training, and community home visits. She has never lost that perspective: Christian first, doctor second.

It is very busy, but she loves it. Laughing, she says, "People who thrive on routine cannot survive in family medicine because it's so many things at once!"

Recently, one of the interns called Belyse to ask about a patient he was treating. He wasn't sure what was wrong with him or what to do. The patient was anxious and unable to sleep. When Belyse asked the reason, the intern revealed that the patient was afraid. All his friends had passed away, and this elderly man in his seventies was afraid he would be next.

Belyse told the intern, "This is an emergency."

"What do you mean an emergency?" The intern was confused. "He's stable. His vital signs are all good."

"This is an emergency," Belyse insisted. "This man needs to get born again. He's tormented by sin and fear of death. That is an indication for a salvation kind of prescription."

Not only did renewing her faith encourage Belyse to be able to keep going, but it redefined almost everything, including the definition of an emergency.

GOD HAS CONFUSED SCIENCE

This redefinition of purpose has Dr. Belyse on the lookout for how God is moving in and among her patients. Soon after that reorienting time, she met a patient who was thirty-seven weeks pregnant and who had arrived at the hospital with complications. Upon admitting her, Belyse learned this was not her first pregnancy. It was her fifth, but she did not have a living child.

Throughout that busy night, though her relatives were rude and demanding, this mother was calm and composed, not talking at all.

That night her baby was delivered by Cesarean section. Belyse was not scheduled to work the next day, but she could not get this mother off her mind. *Had the baby survived? How was the mother?*

God kept prompting her to go to the hospital to check on this mother. And that evening, she was heartbroken to learn that the baby had died. With a heavy heart, and uncertain of any words that she could say, Belyse found the mother. The mother was acting strong and not bothered, but Belyse could tell that she, too, was heartbroken. Belyse grabbed the mother's hand and said, "I will pray with you now. And I'll continue to pray with you until God gives you a child."

They shared contact information, and the woman was discharged. But in the coming months, whenever she had a question, she'd reach out to Belyse. And over the course of the next two years, she suffered another loss, this time due to an ectopic pregnancy.

One day Belyse randomly got a burden to pray for this woman. They had not spoken recently, so there was nothing specific on her mind, but she was compelled to pray . . . and pray and pray and pray.

As it turned out, this mother had conceived again, and at thirty-two weeks, she returned to the hospital in premature labor.

Belyse was working that night in pediatrics. When she received the premature baby into her care, again she was compelled to pray, "Lord, this baby has to live."

Her prayers were insistent.

"Lord, this is Africa. You know how important it is for this woman and her marriage to have a child. Please. Let this one live."

The tiny infant fought infections and other issues that go along with prematurity, but eventually, both mother and baby went home—healthy and whole. As of this writing, that mother now has two living children.

And the lesson for Belyse? God uses prayer to make a difference. As a doctor, she uses science and all the medical skills she has studied so hard to learn. And as a child of God, she uses prayer and spiritual discernment. When it comes to treating patients, both are critically important to the way Belyse practices medicine.

On a different occasion during her training, Belyse received a six-year-old child who had epilepsy. Despite being on every available medication, he was continuously seizing. Nothing was helping. He was even put on a ventilator in combination with the strong medications, and nothing was working.

After a week of continuous seizing, the physicians decided that even if he were to stop seizing right then, his brain would be irreparably damaged. So the family met and agreed it was best to discontinue care. The child would be removed from the ventilator and allowed to pass. The family was moved to a more private room, and the waiting began.

Belyse was working on call that weekend, but it was a very busy day, and she wasn't in the room the whole day. But in the evening, when the rest of the hospital quieted down, she went to check on the family. To her surprise, the child was sitting up. The boy, who was supposed to be dying, was back to his baseline in every way.

Belyse thought to herself, *Wow. God has literally confused science here.*

Everyone was expecting this child to die, but he did not.

In some ways, being a doctor actually makes it harder to have faith because you know the natural progression of disease. You know what is going to happen. If the kidneys are failing, you expect certain things to happen. If you have this certain kind of tumor, you have six months to live. But sometimes God alters that path. He can change the trajectory of disease. The Bible says that Jesus is the same yesterday, today, and forever (Hebrews 13:8). While He was on earth, Jesus healed people—even those whom doctors had been unable to help—and He can still do so today.

Belyse is always careful to tell patients, "This is what science says. This is the scientific prognosis. But I am not God . . . and we always want to leave room for God to surprise and confuse us."

Of course, God does not always heal. Things don't always work out the way we think they should. Sometimes illnesses *do* follow the expected trajectory. But even then, the hand of God is evident in people's pain.

On a recent pediatric call, Belyse encountered a nine-month-old baby with an untreatable genetic condition that was incompatible with life. Even as they made a plan to de-escalate care and remove the baby from the ventilator, Belyse, in faith, prayed, "Lord, can You do something? Can You heal this baby? The science has stopped. Our medicine is no help. So this is where You can surprise us. Will You confuse the science and heal this baby?"

As a mother of young children herself, she could imagine the pain of saying goodbye to a child you have breastfed and cared for for nine months. The baby's mother was composed.

"I have accepted that if this is the will of God that my baby will pass on, then so be it."

Belyse agreed. But deep down in her heart, she had faith that the baby would actually be healed—that God would perform a miracle.

They prayed together, and Belyse left her hospital room thinking this baby was not going to die.

And the baby did not die that Friday night.

But on Monday, when she went back to work, she saw the report: the baby had died over the weekend.

She was heartbroken. *Why, God? Where are You in all this sadness?*

But then she remembered the grieving mother's words, rejoicing that this child's twin was still alive and that she had the comfort of God and the support of her husband even in her pain.

The mother had shared a room with eight other women in the hospital while her baby was in the ICU. The other women kept asking her, "What is happening in your marriage? Why are you so supportive of each other? So loving? We don't see this anywhere nowadays."

And that grieving mother explained to Dr. Belyse that though she was heartbroken to lose her baby, she was still able to see the hand of God accomplishing something good.

And Belyse knew it was true. Even in heartbreak, God was still at work.

FOLLOW ME AS I FOLLOW CHRIST

Belyse doesn't really see herself as a teacher. Nevertheless, she finds herself committed to teaching and mentoring interns and residents as a way to expand kingdom-minded healthcare in Africa. Christian doctors who are trained in all the scientific specifics of healthcare but are also conscious of what God is doing among them are able to spread the love of God to patients throughout the country and continent. As they train others to do what they are doing, the environment changes.

And like a small candle in the darkness, the light spreads.

When Belyse joined the program for family medicine in the hospital, it was under the direction of a missionary doctor from the United Kingdom. But as he recognized the different strengths of each of the residents, he encouraged them to take ownership.

One of the residents who was interested in teaching and training now serves as faculty. The missionary doctor is there to support and guide, but he intentionally handed the program over to the national who was trained with the support of MedSend.

The MedSend National Scholars program model is changing medicine in Africa and elsewhere. There is an intentional shift to encourage nationals who have received these kinds of scholarships to train others to serve as doctors and to step into leadership positions that impact and inspire their fellow workers.

INSIGHT, WISDOM, AND TAKEAWAYS

As Belyse reflects on her life, she sees how God has been writing her story and orchestrating all things to work out for her good. She is committed to using her training in family medicine to expand His kingdom.

God is generous and can provide all things for free, but she finds herself frequently asking if there is something specific He wants her to do or somewhere specific He wants her to go. She prays her life will be a seed that will bear much fruit.

Her advice to fellow believers: Acknowledge that God is in your story. In response to His kindness and generosity, seek His purpose for your life. You never know how far a small seed of obedience can reach. You never know the multiplication He will do with your life.

How will you let Him use you?

CHAPTER 9

FAITH LELEI

FULL CIRCLE

Ten-year-old Faith Lelei lay on her stomach, head propped in her hands, eyes glued to the television. Watching the half-hour *700 Club* program on the Kenyan national television channel was part of her daily routine.

On this day the program featured Christian missionary doctors holding medical camps in African villages. It was interesting to see what they were doing, and her heart was glad people were getting help, but she couldn't help but wonder, *Why? Why must people come all the way from overseas to treat people in my country? And why would they do that? What's driving them?*

Faith's family was middle class. She got an education without too much stress. She did not go to sleep hungry. She and her family had all the basics and a few of what some would consider luxuries. But her father had spent his life working in areas of hardship, coordinating relief and trying to relieve human suffering.

As a young girl, it bothered her to know there were those in her very own community going to sleep hungry. So watching television that day, she thought, *Is there some way I could help be a solution to the needs in my community? Could I do what these white doctors are doing?*

As she grew up, she continued to consider how she might serve others, perhaps in the areas of community development, agribusiness, and food security. As born-again Christians, Faith's parents brought her up in the church, taught her the Word of God, and showed her how to pray. She grew up knowing that however she might serve others, it would certainly be tied to serving God.

She also loved music, and after high school, she seriously considered going on for further musical education in South Africa. But when the time came to make a decision, as she was praying, she felt a quiet conviction—not a voice, just a quiet conviction—that she should pursue medicine, not music. Somehow she knew it was from the Lord, so she changed directions. God confirmed her leading by providing the necessary finances. She was able to live at home, and amazingly, she discovered that the place where her father was working at the time would pay seventy percent of her tuition for the duration of medical school.

A VISION REFINED

In medical school, she was part of a Christian community group that ended up being life-changing in helping her refine her life calling and purpose. Together the young people explored what God wanted them to do.

What is the Great Commission? And could they marry that with the Great Commandment? By the time she was done with medical school, Faith felt very clearly that God had directed her toward medicine purely as an instrument to send His love.

An internship at faith-based Kijabe Hospital allowed her to interact with other Christian colleagues and practice in daily ways what it meant to serve God as a doctor. Most of the physicians were from the West.

Again, she wondered, *What makes one a missionary? Is it that they are a person of white skin? Is it that they have traveled far? Is a missionary one who is fundraising? I also am serving God . . .*

At the end of her internship, she took a position in a thirty-bed rural hospital as the only physician. There were several physician assistants, but she was the only doctor. The hospital had an operating theater where she did Cesarean sections and other minor surgeries, and she was also responsible for a large HIV clinic with two thousand outpatients. It was a sink-or-swim kind of situation where she had to trust God moment by moment.

One time she was treating a pregnant patient who required a Cesarean section. Unfortunately, the patient had a condition called placenta accreta, wherein the placenta adheres to the uterine wall instead of detaching and delivering after the baby. The only thing that can save the mother's life is surgically removing the uterus.

Faith had assisted in a similar procedure during her internship but had never been the primary surgeon. With a deep breath, she drew upon all she remembered and asked God to guide her hands. Somehow, God enabled her to remember the steps, and she was able to remove the uterus, despite the patient bleeding profusely and requiring CPR three times while on the operating table. The patient left the hospital alive, and it was clear to Faith this was God's work, not hers.

Other times the results were not as positive, like the time she lost a nine-month-old baby because the hospital did not have adequate oxygen supplies and equipment. He came in on a Saturday morning after having been struggling to breathe the entire night. Faith tried to resuscitate him so he could be referred to another facility, since they didn't have an oxygen plant at her small hospital, and their purchased oxygen cylinders were empty. While gathering everything for transporting the child, he died in the ambulance. Faith still remembers his face and his name.

God, this is not the way it's supposed to be. It just isn't.

Those bad days of mourning and loss were tempered by good days of feeling like she was making a difference, like the days she would go to local high schools to provide talks on sex education and HIV. Or the days she went to women's meetings in the village to educate them about Pap smears, cervical cancer screenings, and other women's health issues.

As the village doctor, she became a fixture in the community. The lady she bought vegetables from was her patient. The seamstress who would stitch her clothes was her patient. Her cobbler was her patient. Going to the market, she'd hear, "Ah, Doctor! Doctor!" . . . and often would come home with an extra banana or two in her basket.

All the while, God was forming her heart toward being a doctor focused on sharing compassion. For example, one time she had three patients who had multidrug-resistant tuberculosis.

How do you show compassion to someone from whom you need to be isolating? How do you touch a patient yet protect yourself?

Faith had many geriatric patients and ended up doing a lot of end-of-life and palliative care. She enjoyed sitting down with patients, ensuring they were comfortable, and having hard discussions with their families.

She always prayed with them, asking, "Do you know the Lord?"

She was able to see God heal some on earth, and many were healed completely by transitioning to glory.

It was a mix of harrowing and happy. And through it all, the Lord opened her eyes to the value of family medicine. If she was going to serve in a rural place as the only medical person in a hundred-kilometer radius, then what would equip her the most? What further training would best equip her to follow God's calling?

Through a series of events, she became aware of a family practice residency program at a mission hospital in Kenya.

Thanks to a stipend from the MedSend National Scholars Program, she was able to complete that training. One of the biggest blessings of that financial support was that she could focus on her education without the pressure of working another job at night to pay for the education. And it gave her affirmation that this education was worth pursuing in her quest to be the type of physician who lives out her life and calling in the way that God has asked.

COVID

Faith's first full-time position after residency was in an administrative role to set up a quality and patient-safety department for a hospital. It's not that the hospital didn't care about quality and patient safety before she got there, but there wasn't a coordinated, structured effort. Her job requirements involved looking at five different areas: quality improvement, quality assurance and accreditation, credentialing of doctors, clinical ethics, and infection control and outbreak.

This was a huge task, but thankfully, she'd had some measure of experience at the rural hospital when the hospital administrator was relieved of his position and Faith was asked to fill in. Providing hospital leadership while also being the only primary doctor was a huge learning curve, but that experience proved to be invaluable as she tackled these five areas of responsibility.

Just as she was getting up to speed and taking control over the infection control and outbreak management, word began to circulate about an unknown virus that was spreading rapidly all over the world—the virus that causes COVID-19.

Some of the leadership and political management muscles she had developed as a fill-in administrator at that rural hospital were soon stretched to the limits as she was called to lead and run the hospital's COVID response. Their hospital had the largest COVID center in the country but had very little information about the virus—just like everywhere else in the world.

Faith found herself night after night poring over whatever information she could get her hands on. What is the CDC saying? What is the WHO saying? What are the guidelines? What are the *new* guidelines? And the biggest challenge was, everything she read applied to resource-rich locations. In Kenya, she didn't have access to masks or gowns or vaccines. How did the guidelines translate to her unique situation?

She had a team, but the weight to lead was on her. And the weight was immense.

When Kenya confirmed its first COVID-19 patient on June 4, 2020, and they needed to have medical personnel working the isolation units, Faith felt like it was up to her to demonstrate that they could do it. They could take care of very sick COVID patients with love and compassion, even if they were expecting them to die. So they began a rotation of doctors working in the COVID unit, with Faith leading the way.

The Friday before she was to work her first shift in the COVID unit, she went to the open-air market and bought what was perhaps an irrational amount of food—food that would last her family six weeks to three months . . . in case she died. By this time, Faith had a husband and two small children. She wanted to relieve her husband of the burden of looking for food if he was in the unthinkable position of trying to hold their little family together.

If I die, at least they will have food. This is one thing I can control.

Children are perceptive, and Faith didn't realize how much her children were taking in until one day her six-year-old asked, "Mommy, will you die?"

She told him, "We pray that God takes care of me. And because I know the Lord, if I do die, I will go to heaven. And your daddy will take good care of you. But I would be very sad if I do not get to be your mommy anymore."

There is no script anywhere for having these conversations with your children.

The situation at the hospital was unbelievably stressful. There were heartbreaking moments when the COVID ward would be full and they would have to refer a patient somewhere else, knowing there was nowhere for them to go. Oxygen turned out to be the limiting factor, not only for their hospital, but for the whole country. Sometimes there would be physical room for a patient but no more oxygen for treating them, so they simply couldn't take in one more patient.

There were so many difficult decisions. If they were prioritizing oxygen usage, how did they do that? Younger over older? What were the guidelines? Communicating those decisions meant answering so many heart-wrenching questions and having so many tough conversations. The pressure of leading in these uncertain, life-and-death situations was heavy.

Heaving a big sigh, Faith recalled, "Looking back at that time, I tell God, 'I pray I never have to do that ever again in my life. That none of us will.'"

Faith leaned heavily on her hospital team during that time. They waded through the fire together. A Bible study with fellow staff members proved to be a lifeline. Even when it was not advised for groups to meet together, they found a way to meet outdoors, spread apart. They could be vulnerable with each other—admitting how hard it all was, laughing together, and crying out to God.

After a couple of years, as the pandemic was dying down, Faith took on new responsibility when she began working as the director of clinical services at her hospital. Though different from leading the COVID response, this position also came with heavy responsibility.

Faith was put in charge of all clinical services: delivery, theater services, inpatient and outpatient services, diagnostics, physio, nutrition, and radiology. Even the morgue was her business. It was a big task, and she found herself seeking God's guidance every day, every hour, and sometimes even every minute.

Not wanting to give up patient care entirely, Faith now spends eighty percent of her time in hospital administration and twenty percent in active patient care. This allows her to still interact with patients as well as keep in touch with what is actually going on in the hospital.

YOUR GOD LOVES WOMEN

As Faith interacts with patients and coworkers, sharing the love of Christ is always at the forefront of her mind. She knows it's possible to be a good doctor without being a Christian. So what sets a Christian doctor apart? She says it's intentionally sharing the love of Christ. Not just love and compassion in general, but specifically, the love of Christ—in words and actions. She says it's easy at faith-based hospitals like Kijabe to assume the patient will hear about Jesus simply because of the environment. Surely someone will tell them, or they'll hear it on the television. Because the Christian presence is strong, you assume someone will do it, but that often means no one is doing it.

But even simple things make an impact when done with intention.

One time Faith was taking care of a Muslim woman.

Faith asked, "How is your faith helping you cope with your current illness?"

As they talked, Faith shared that she is a Christian and that she can ask the Lord for help when she's in such a situation.

The conversation was simple—not more than two minutes. But as this Muslim lady left the clinic, she remarked, "One thing I love about you Christians is that your God loves you. Your God loves women."

Faith told her, "Yes, and my God loves you too."

Faith no longer has contact with this woman, but she still prays for her.

God, will You show Your love to that woman? Will You remember her and seek her out? Show her that You do love women, including her.

As a Christian doctor, Faith wants to notice and act during these small moments. Not everyone is going to give their lives to Christ in her clinic. She knows this. That part is ultimately not her responsibility. There is a vulnerability that comes with illness that often opens people to seek hope. She wants to be sensitive to that. She believes what should set her apart from any other good and excellent physician is the ability to take note of what God is saying.

> *Is this the correct time? Is this the person you'd like me to speak to about the love of Christ? What is the one sentence that would be most helpful?*

This takes walking with God daily. It takes asking Him at the moment, even in the administrative work, *How can I best honor You in all these decisions? How can I support my colleagues? How does my conduct point people to Christ even there?*

PARTNERS IN MINISTRY

When Faith began her medical training, there were many more Westerners than African nationals in leadership. But that balance has begun to shift. And the big game changer? Training.

Faith says the Western missionaries have been intentional in pushing for training surgeons and family physicians. Their foresight to put in the hours to create the training programs and get them up and running is immense. Many are still involved in training, but people like Faith are starting to take leadership roles. In fact, in her current role as clinical services director, Faith is now the manager of some of the missionaries who initially trained her.

As more and more nationals graduate from residency training programs and join leadership teams, they are able to direct the priorities according to the unique needs of the community. Westerners and nationals are becoming partners, progressing beyond what Faith would have described a few years ago as a parent-child relationship. It's a time of transition, and Faith says they need both.

"We continue to share knowledge with one another. We sharpen one another. We support one another. I think we still need one another. So I hope to continue to see that relationship growing and that partnering relationship continuing to happen. As medical professionals, and especially as brothers and sisters in Christ, we need each other."

As the hospital leadership team looks to the future, Faith says the goal and question remain the same: How do we impact lives to the glory of God through healthcare and education?

INSIGHT, WISDOM, AND TAKEAWAYS

Ten-year-old Faith asked the question "What does it mean to be a missionary?" She and her husband are living their lives as an answer. It has nothing to do with the color of their skin or the distance they travel. It has to do with the willingness of their hearts to follow God's call.

Faith's husband, an orthopedic doctor with seminary training, spends part of his time doing clinical work but the bulk of his time in ministry. He started a missions organization called Medical Missions Africa, which recruits, mobilizes, trains, and fundraises for local missionaries to serve among unreached people groups in Kenya and throughout Africa.

As a family, they've been amazed at what God can do with willing people, even with limited resources. In all the places they've had missionaries, there is revival. People want to hear the Word of God.

The Lelei family's prayer is that God would multiply that work.

What else might He ask of them? They don't know, but they'll be ready when He does.

CHAPTER 10

PERRY JANSEN

PARTNERS IN HOPE

Perry Jansen was frustrated. As a family physician in a semirural community practice, he got to do a bit of everything. He liked delivering babies, fixing broken bones, and doing minor surgeries. He enjoyed his patients, and this was the kind of work he wanted to do.

So why the frustration? He blamed the increasing red tape in the American medical system and financial political issues in the local practice, but there was also something just under the surface that he couldn't quite put his finger on.

He'd become quite involved in his church, and as he grew in his faith, he kept wondering if there was something more or different that he was supposed to be doing. Was there a way he could serve God or serve those who didn't know God in a more specific way? Should he leave medicine and pursue ministry? Maybe as a pastor? He wasn't sure.

One day, driving home from work, Perry was compelled to pull over. Parking next to a sparkling river, sun glinting through the trees, Perry began to pray.

"Lord, I'll do whatever You want me to. I just don't know if I can keep going like this for much longer."

He felt the Lord reply: *Just pay attention. Keep your eyes open.*

That evening Perry and his wife, Brenda, went to a friend's birthday party. It just so happened that the friend had grown up in Malawi, and his parents had just come back from serving at a Bible college there. That Bible college had built a medical clinic, but they were in a bind. The doctor from the United States who was supposed to come to run the clinic wasn't coming after all. They were looking for a replacement doctor.

Perry and Brenda looked at each other.

I wonder . . . Okay, Lord, we're paying attention.

That encounter led to Perry taking a short-term trip to Malawi to assist with installing an X-ray machine. They figured they should at least visit the country and get a feel for the place as a way of discerning if God might be calling them there.

Perry saw the hospital. He saw the city, and he wondered, *Can I really bring my family here?*

He also recognized two possible roadblocks. There were tropical diseases and conditions that he simply didn't know anything about. He would definitely need tropical medicine training. He'd need to address the significant debt load they already had from his medical school tuition.

Meanwhile, Brenda was at home reading a biography of a missionary doctor who had been called to the jungles of Gabon. His stories were crazy—and inspiring. By the time Perry returned, Brenda was convinced God was calling them to be healthcare missionaries to Malawi.

Upon his return, Perry learned that his medical practice was consolidating for financial reasons and closing the clinic where he worked. He'd be required to move to a location he didn't prefer. It felt like further confirmation:

This is no longer the place for you. I want you somewhere else.

After praying and discussing with Brenda, Perry resigned from his position, giving the clinic a six-month notice. And then things began to happen quickly.

They found and were accepted by a sending organization; they connected with MedSend to address the debt issue, and they sold their house, cars, and most of their belongings. All in all, it was seven months from the night they began to wonder "what if" to the time they were fully supported and packing their bags for tropical medicine training.

PEOPLE IN PAIN

In addition to his training as a doctor, Perry and Brenda had walked through some intense personal trials that uniquely positioned them to face what was to come in Malawi.

During Perry's third year of medical school, Brenda had become pregnant with their first child. Baby Mallory was born with severe heart deformities and almost died at birth. On the first day of her life, she had two surgeries—temporary fixes to get the blood flowing in the right direction. Then at six months old, she underwent a risky corrective surgery. She was in intensive care for about eight weeks and had heart, kidney, and liver failure—but amazingly survived.

As her heart started getting better and she began recovering from the surgery, they realized she'd suffered severe brain damage. When they took her home, it was as if she was starting life over as a newborn. Her progress was nothing short of amazing.

A year after discharge, her neurologist said that though two-thirds of her brain had been damaged from low oxygen levels, the damage was barely identifiable. If you weren't looking for it, you wouldn't notice it.

During this challenging time, Perry and Brenda naturally had a lot of questions—questions for the medical professionals, but maybe more significantly, questions for God.

Why? Why does God allow suffering? How could this be His plan for Mallory and their family?

As they focused on caring for Mallory and her physical heart, they found God working in their spiritual hearts. They saw again and again that He was in control. He didn't guarantee there wouldn't be suffering but was always with them in their pain and confusion.

The following years included the installation of a pacemaker and many medical appointments. She did fairly well until age five, when she developed heart failure. Her compromised little heart was no longer meeting the needs of her growing body. She began to decline and came close to death as they waited at home for a heart transplant.

But once she received a new heart, the transformation was amazing. She went from a chronically ill, skinny, barely breathing little girl to a robust, active little girl running around. The medications gave her a big, puffy face and hairy eyebrows, but she was full of vim and vigor. For thirteen months, she did really well. And then, suddenly, she became very sick. She was in school on a Friday, went to the hospital on Sunday, and sadly, passed away on Monday. Her body simply rejected the new heart.

Again, God was near to Perry and Brenda in their grief and sorrow. They had to come to terms with the fact that God doesn't always do what we want Him to do. Suffering comes to people. It's a part of life, and it isn't God's failure. God does things through pain and failure and loss that He couldn't do otherwise.

God surrounded them with His love in the form of family and friends and a church community. The body of Christ held them up in their pain.

This experience left them and their faith forever changed.

Perry says, "We both have an affinity for people who are in pain, whether through loss or health."

They couldn't have known it at the time, but God was uniquely preparing them to serve in very painful circumstances in Malawi—painful circumstances that involved loss, grief, and death.

WHAT BREAKS YOUR HEART

When Perry moved his family to Malawi in 2000, he knew HIV/AIDS was a huge issue, but until he started treating patients, he didn't realize just how devastating it was.

Reading about the issue in the news was nothing compared to sitting knee-to-knee with someone with all the signs of HIV/AIDS and knowing the treatment options were severely limited. As an American doctor, Perry's instinct was to diagnose and immediately begin treatment. But there wasn't any treatment for HIV in

Africa at that time—at least not affordable treatment. HIV was basically a hopeless death sentence.

This wasn't the first time Perry had faced this illness. Though he hadn't encountered much HIV/AIDS in his semirural family practice, he'd seen this disease during residency at a UCLA-affiliated community hospital in Los Angeles a decade before. The large gay community there was facing staggering numbers of HIV diagnoses, and there were no treatments.

The lack of information about the disease, lack of treatment options, and the sheer number of difficult, complex cases meant that many patients got assigned to residents like Perry. He saw a lot of illness and late-stage AIDS. His residency was marked by taking care of patients with a new disease for which no one had much experience and very few tools.

Ten years later, the situation in Malawi felt similar: many patients with late-stage HIV and limited options for treatment. Perry found that his instinctive "diagnose and treat" protocol wasn't going to work here.

He wrestled with whether or not it was even beneficial to test someone for HIV, knowing it would likely mean they would simply return to their village to die. He struggled with giving a death sentence over and over again. He found that unless the patient had a very strong support system in place, a gentler approach was better.

He'd see them for several weeks in a row, saying, "You seem to be having some weakness in your immune system."

He would treat them with antibiotics, try to improve their nutrition with supplements and vitamins, and try to stimulate their immune system. But in a very real sense, his focus became trying to help his patients die with dignity.

It was exhausting and emotionally draining, to say the least.

One day, while listening to Christian radio, Perry heard the words to a Scott Krippayne song:

I want to see the world the way You do
What breaks Your heart?
What makes You cry?
What would I see
If I looked through Your eyes?
I want to grow closer and closer to You
'Til what breaks Your heart
Will break mine too.

In those moments, as the words of this song reverberated, he sensed God confirming that this was the pain he'd been called to. This was the need he had been prepared to meet. His exhaustion and heartache was a small reflection of what God must be feeling, but it was magnified toward the whole epidemic. This season helped him recognize his true calling.

Caring for HIV patients became his passion and the focus of his career.

Shortly after he had arrived in Malawi, Perry had been introduced to the head of UNAIDS, the United Nations agency responsible for the AIDS response. He joined a group of experts meeting with the national Ministry of Health to decide if Malawi would ever be able to administer antiretroviral therapies. They were becoming much more effective and possibly more cost-effective.

Perry began using them in his own clinic. With the support of churches from the United States, he was able to get generic antiretroviral medications from India. And he began to see an amazing impact. Rather than just watching people decline and eventually die, he observed they were getting better. He'd treat their infection, and they'd get a bit stronger, gain weight, and within several months be back to work.

He and his colleagues eventually started a program that allowed many people to get treatment very quickly and saw a dramatic reduction in deaths from HIV. Their program led the way for developing countries to also deal more effectively with HIV.

As a doctor, those kinds of results were addicting, especially when he'd seen the trajectory of the disease without treatment. It was these results that motivated Perry to start a new organization focused specifically on HIV treatment.

PARTNERS IN HOPE

Perry had a vision for a clinic dedicated entirely to treating the sickest HIV patients. He knew he couldn't do it alone. With several Malawian colleagues, connections from the Ministry of Health, a local pastor, and a local organizational consultant, he formed a board, developed a vision and mission statement, and officially registered as a local nongovernmental organization (NGO).

They had no US entity, but they did have the full support of one of the Jansens' partnering churches in California. They had a Malawian friend who was a real estate agent.

She told them, "I have this former IV fluids factory over on the bad side of town. It's been for sale for seven years. I'm not sure it's ever going to sell. Do you want to take a look at it?"

A former factory on the bad side of town didn't sound like much of a clinic, but with nothing to lose, they went to look at it.

Stepping onto the property, Perry immediately began to imagine: *This could be the reception area. The clinic could be here. X-ray and lab and inpatient services here. Man, this building would be amazing.*

They were able to negotiate an unbelievable price and then had money leftover to renovate. Perry recruited a couple of other missionary doctors, and within a year, they were seeing patients in the new clinic.

In time the clinic came to include a general clinic, inpatient ward, HIV and AIDS clinic, pharmacy, and counseling center. With amazing facilities and first-rate infectious disease specialists, Partners in Hope also provides support to other health facilities in nine districts in the country.

Over the years, patient stories continued to break Perry's heart. A woman came to the clinic with a severely suppressed immune system, tuberculosis in her lungs, and sepsis—infection throughout her whole body. This woman had run away from an abusive father at age thirteen and ended up in commercial sex work. She had three children from unknown fathers and, of course, contracted HIV. As she recovered in the clinic, she shared how God had used her near-death time to draw her to Himself.

She was watching a televangelist on TV, and God spoke to her, completely transforming her life. She survived the infection and now has her own ministry working with prostitutes, educating and encouraging them toward other careers, but also sharing Christ and discipling them.

One of her sons also ended up being HIV positive. At age eight, he came to the clinic and asked to be tested.

"I'm here to be tested because my mom has HIV, and I think I have it too. I need the medicines that she's on."

That son is now a young man and works as an accountant.

When Perry and Brenda returned to the United States, they left the organization in the capable hands of Malawian colleagues. The CEO, COO, board chairman, medical director, and programs director are all Malawian. With support from the United States (USAID/PEPFAR) and the University of California, Los Angeles (UCLA), the Partners in Hope HIV treatment program now reaches over 200,000 HIV patients in over 130 facilities with free, life-saving treatment.

Perry stays in touch, calling once a month to provide encouragement and coaching. It gives him great joy to see the fruit of Westerners and nationals working together.

INSIGHT, WISDOM, AND TAKEAWAYS

Perry's work as a doctor in Africa has deepened his view on the theological aspects of what the church should be doing and what the kingdom of God looks like—more than just signing people up for your faith.

Looking to Christ as an example, Perry has come to believe that the true kingdom of God is something you're living out. Jesus spent His time healing, touching, preaching, and being with people—demonstrating what the kingdom should look like. Living out the kingdom now means caring for the poor, caring for the sick, and loving people.

The Lord's Prayer says, "Your will be done on Earth as it is in Heaven." That means that what we're doing now is an imperfect reflection of what ultimately will be perfection. We don't know when that perfection will be. But we don't wait.

We keep our eyes open, pay attention, and do what we can when God calls us.

CHAPTER 11

GEOFFREY MOSES

HEALING HANDS AND SPIRITUAL AWAKENING

Sierra Leone has some of the worst healthcare statistics in the world. The West African country consistently ranks among the top for infant mortality and death of children under five. In recent years it has also made the list of top worst places on earth for a young girl to grow up because of genital mutilation, early marriage, harsh living conditions, and difficult cultural expectations.

Dr. Geoffrey Moses has seen and heard a lot of things in his years in Sierra Leone as a family physician. But there is one thing he's not heard. In almost five years, he has yet to take a pregnancy history from any woman who has kept all her pregnancies, delivered all her children, and is holding all her children alive today. Every single woman he sees for prenatal or OB-GYN care tells the story of the loss of a child (or children), multiple pregnancies, or . . . the curse of infertility.

Suffering is a way of life. And it's not just the women. A lack of clean water, proper food resources, education about hygiene, and an extreme shortage of medical facilities and trained medical personnel affect men, women, and children alike.

Malaria, tuberculosis, and HIV are equal opportunity diseases. And so is Ebola. From 2014 to 2016, Sierra Leone, along with Guinea and Liberia, was severely hit by the most widespread Ebola virus disease epidemic in history.

This just so happened to be when Geoffrey was finishing up his medical residency. And it just so happened to be the time when God was confirming that Geoffrey should serve Him as a medical missionary.

At a time when many others were *leaving* Africa, when others would not want anything to do with living in a place like Sierra Leone, Geoffrey felt God *calling* him to go. To make a difference. To use his skills. And to use them in Sierra Leone, of all places.

A RIGHTEOUS ANGER

Though you and I might have to pull up a map of Africa and search for a while before we find Sierra Leone, Geoffrey grew up hearing about the country from his father. His father is Sierra Leonean and as a young man immigrated to Canada to pursue higher education. In time he met and married Geoffrey's mother, a Canadian with a Mennonite farming background.

That cross-cultural marriage and resulting family life shaped Geoffrey's view of the world and his own place in it. It made him quite adaptable to different situations and cultures. A naturally empathetic and compassionate person, he found himself easily accepting people regardless of their background or personality. He could mingle and be comfortable in a wide array of different people groups.

Naturally, Geoffrey's father told stories of his childhood in Sierra Leone, but what Geoffrey mainly remembers is hearing his parents' distressed conversations about war.

For over ten years, from 1991 to 2002, Sierra Leone underwent a violent civil war sometimes referred to as the Blood Diamond Feud. Between 50,000 and 70,000 people died, 2.5 million people were displaced, and the country was set back many years in development. The conflict was marked by life-altering atrocities—rapes, mutilations, and the forced use of child soldiers. Geoffrey remembers his father being glued to the television, trying to recognize faces, trying to see if any of those he had left behind were still alive. Geoffrey saw the pictures—piles of bodies, chaos, and violence—and he heard his father speculating whether any of his family members were among them.

This terrible tragedy is what God used to begin to grow a passion within Geoffrey. It was a small seed, but the desire grew. He wanted to help the less fortunate, those living in extreme poverty, and those with little hope for their futures.

Geoffrey was always disciplined in his studies, but as he progressed through school, he felt a growing motivation, a growing righteous anger. He wanted to bring justice and light into the world. He wanted to serve God and be a part of bringing about the redemption of mankind.

He loved animals and for a while thought he might want to be a vet. But as he matured in his faith, that small seed flourished into a desire to serve people. And he wanted to do it by bringing the gospel to unreached people groups through the delivery of healthcare. He wanted to offer hope in places like he'd seen on the television—places in darkness and despair.

Even as he began medical school, he had overseas service on his heart. In fact, in his first conversation with Nicole, the woman who would become his wife, he declared that he felt like God was calling him to serve in Africa. Nicole, an occupational therapy student, somehow ended up asking Geoffrey to take her with him. And he had a bit of a light bulb moment: *Is this my future wife?*

Over the next few years, their relationship developed, and God continued to confirm his calling on their lives. In the upside-down way of God's kingdom, it was the Ebola epidemic that sealed the deal. They both felt such empathy and pain for those going through that crisis that they knew God was confirming that Sierra Leone was the place and healthcare was the vehicle.

HEALING

Today Geoffrey and Nicole, along with their four children, live in a small, impoverished community outside the capital city of Sierra Leone.

Geoffrey runs an outpatient clinic, serving people who have little other access to healthcare. In fact, in the whole country, there are only a handful of doctors—less than one per 50,000 people. You can imagine that as word of Geoffrey's clinic spread, the patients started coming.

Most come without a penny to their name, hoping for care and relief from their suffering. Many then travel to their home villages, sometimes for days, to collect family members or friends with long-term suffering and unmanageable conditions. In the absence of trained medical personnel, they've sought treatment in the form of traditional practices from herbalists, witch doctors, or secret society members, often without finding relief. The care and follow-up from a physician like Geoffrey is a compelling reason to travel.

As word spread, more affluent people from the city also came out to his clinic, seeking Geoffrey's Western medical training and diagnostic skills.

Nicole sees patients as she's able, in between her full-time schedule of home educating their four children. As a pediatric occupational therapist, she treats children with disabilities.

Both Geoffrey and Nicole also hand out a healthy dose of spiritual hope. As they attempt to offer physical healing, they are ever aware that people's true need is for spiritual awakening.

In his medical training, Geoffrey saw an attempt to separate matters of faith from physical healing, but the more patients he treats, the more he's convinced that is impossible. God created people with mind, body, and spirit. The Bible says we are fearfully and wonderfully made. There are complexities in the human experience that are only understood by our Creator, but the overlap between the physical and the spiritual cannot be ignored. As a doctor with a strong faith, his goal is to bridge the gap—to help patients see the connection between beliefs and their mental wellness, behavioral health, and overall well-being.

In a country like Sierra Leone, he is painfully aware that he is often dealing with matters of life and death. Geoffrey is able to connect quickly and deeply with his patients, expressing concern and care for both their bodies and souls.

With such limited medical services and high mortality rates, he always points patients toward eternity. Whether patients live one day or one hundred years on earth, it's all just a blink of an eye compared to the scope of eternity.

Often he will say, "Let's pray. We are going to pray for a miracle. And we're also going to pray for your spiritual eyes to be opened. Because the biggest miracle of all is not physical healing but that the truth and revelation of Jesus Christ would be revealed in your heart."

This is the core of Geoffrey and Nicole's ministry: striking a balance of healing and preaching. They alleviate pain and suffering here on earth. And even if it's only temporary, a reprieve in physical suffering presents an opportunity to look up and think about the things of God—to think about eternity.

Though they are sometimes able to save children's or adults' lives, they know they can't save anyone spiritually. It has to be a work of God. It's a beautiful, paradoxical miracle that the knowledge of Jesus Christ comes only through spiritual revelation.

So they pray, and they do their part. They heal, and they share the truth.

AN OPEN DOOR

In addition to treating patients at their local clinic, they travel throughout the country offering mobile medical clinics. Many of the villages are in difficult, remote places with terrain requiring four-wheel drive vehicles and a good deal of perseverance, grit, and faith. They've been in some precarious situations and have seen God's hand catch and protect them again and again.

Geoffrey tells about one trip during which they traveled seven hours away from the nearest city. It wasn't as far in miles as you might think, but the mountainous terrain was treacherous, often with no actual road to follow. On that trip Nicole was five months pregnant with their fourth child, and it seemed like the enemy was determined to turn them back.

At one of the clinic sites, Nicole fell off an unfinished building that they were using as a temporary clinic. That easily could have led to harm to both Nicole and the baby, but praise God, she somehow landed properly and protected the child. And that was just the beginning.

As they were finally reaching the village that was their final destination, being guided only by fires on the side of the road, they encountered a tree leaning into the road. In the dark, it almost tore off the whole right passenger door from the hinges, crumpling the side of the vehicle like it was tissue paper. It looked like a large claw had peeled back the metal from the headlight to the door, only narrowly missing the wheel.

Miraculously, the airbag never deployed, protecting Nicole and the unborn baby in the passenger seat. Those instances, coupled with other things that happened on that outreach, solidified what they already knew: the work they were doing was important. There is a spiritual battle, and nothing can harm them unless it passes through the hand of God. He is the one in control of all things.

But why do they do it? Why do they take the risk?

Again, the motivation is twofold: physical healing and spiritual awakening. Geoffrey sees these trips as an opportunity to put his money where his mouth is by blessing, serving, and showing people the love of Jesus through alleviating their physical suffering, regardless of what kind of decisions they make in their faith journey.

They have found that healthcare opens doors that might otherwise be closed. In communities where church-planting missionaries have been chased away or denied access, medical teams are welcomed.

Offering medical services with no strings attached causes a lot of questions.

Why? Why would people come to serve this way? Why are people sacrificing like this?

This is especially true if Geoffrey travels with a team of volunteers from other countries. Most people in the country of Sierra Leone, he says, would gladly trade places with anyone to get a chance at life in another country.

Why would someone choose to come here, to Sierra Leone?

So it's an opportunity to talk about Jesus, to explain that Jesus is more than a prophet. He's the son of the Almighty God. He is divine, and he is the only hope for salvation through his death and resurrection.

They don't force conversion (they know that's only the work of God anyway). They simply "rattle the cage" and cause people to wonder and consider thoughts outside their previous cultural constructs or Islamic mindset.

And it works. They've seen God use the medical outreach trips in really amazing ways, allowing the gospel truth to be shared among people that were previously closed.

In addition to healing physical ailments, alleviating suffering, and prolonging life on earth, there is a spiritual effect that they cannot see with their eyes. There is a spiritual shedding that happens when traditional practices and witchcraft that have been so deeply embedded in the culture begin to be abandoned. It's a power struggle, not against flesh and blood, but against darkness and principalities.

It's nothing short of miraculous. Geoffrey has seen people bring out idols—literal idols, charms, and tools that people had used to practice witchcraft—and burn them.

The joy on their faces and the light of life that comes into their very being when they realize they no longer have to appeal to demons or false gods is overwhelming. No longer do they have to pray enough times during the day or make enough sacrifices to earn favor. They can cease all that striving when they accept the free gift of salvation through Jesus Christ.

That transformation happens from the inside out, and it is amazing to see.

INSIGHT, WISDOM, AND TAKEAWAYS

"Remember, Dr. Moses, the dose is the poison," the doctor of pharmacy cautioned when Geoffrey asked about a particular medication for one of his patients. "Every medicine, if taken in excess, can be bad. And every medicine you need, but take too little of, is not going to help you."

This is practical advice for a doctor, but it has also become a guiding metaphor in Geoffrey's life for adjusting his heart and mind to align with the heart of God.

In a place like Sierra Leone where the need is so great, Geoffrey has found himself scrambling around, putting out many fires, trying to heal the masses . . . and forgetting that even striving toward a good thing is not going to earn him any favor with God. Even something as good as being a doctor and a missionary can become an idol.

If the dose is incorrect—if the good thing replaces seeking God's presence—it becomes a poison. God wants us to obey and abide with Him, not strive.

In an Islamic community, isolated from other believers much of the time, in a place with some of the worst healthcare statistics in the world, Geoffrey and Nicole are learning to lean on the Holy Spirit for guidance in ministry and life.

They are learning to abide.

CHAPTER 12

MICHAEL JOHNSON

D R E A M   B I G

Kay Johnson was dreaming—dreaming of vacation. Her husband, Michael, was about to complete his medical residency program, and they could not wait to celebrate.

After years of undergrad, medical school, and surgical residency, cross-country moves and a growing family, untold long hours and late nights, they had saved their money and were ready for a break.

Kay was dreaming about Hawaii or maybe the Bahamas. Their home cities of Chicago and Philadelphia didn't offer much opportunity for beaches and warm tropical waters. And after all, Michael had said they could go anywhere in the world.

When Michael came home one day and asked, "How would you like to go to Zaire for our vacation?" she was confused.

"Zaire?"

"Yes," he said. "It's warm. It's tropical. It's got dark-skinned people like us."

Kay, ever the good sport, didn't bat an eye. "Okay, tell me more."

Michael explained that he'd been watching a Christian television program that highlighted the need for medical doctors to serve on short-term mission projects. This particular trip was seven weeks in Zaire (now the Democratic Republic of Congo) volunteering in a hospital.

Though they had never discussed missions before, they both felt the Holy Spirit urging them to go. So they made plans for their four children—a generous sister-in-law came to stay—and made their way to Zaire.

In those seven weeks, as they saw patients, interacted with other missionaries, and helped in the clinics as they could despite the language barrier, both Michael and Kay Johnson's hearts were broken for missions. They could not ignore the need in front of them. And they knew they had skills God could use.

BACKGROUND

Michael grew up in Chicago. His parents were divorced when he was young, and his father died from the effects of drug and alcohol use when Michael was thirteen. His mother made a way for him to attend Christian schools, and she always pushed him toward the church. But Michael, like so many other young people, was living his own life when he graduated from high school and began attending Lawrence University in Wisconsin.

He was determined to be a doctor, and the voice of his mother was always in the background reminding him that he was on this earth to be of some service. She had the backing of the church—the African American Christian community at that time had a heavy focus on service. It wasn't enough to simply make money; you also had to be doing some good in the world. Though that was in the background, in college it was definitely not his focus. He was not living that kind of life.

But God has His ways.

One day the Holy Spirit spoke to Michael and said that if he didn't straighten up, he'd live a short life like his father. He was not headed in a good direction. This shook him up enough to make a deal with God:

> *"Look, I'll do whatever You want me to do. I just need a help-meet that will guide me through this."*

Michael transferred to the University of Michigan Medical School, and he started going to church—looking for girls. That's where he eventually met Kay, who would become his wife a couple of years later. After medical school, they moved to Philadelphia so Michael could complete his surgical residency. They added four children to their family, and even though the push to do something good in the world was a quiet hum always in the background, they never, ever talked about missions.

That is, until they started thinking about vacation.

KENYA THROUGH THE BACK DOOR

That vacation turned short-term mission had ramifications they could not have imagined. Though their lives were full—the hours in Michael's surgical practice were still long, family life was certainly busy, and Kay's business was taking off—that trip to Zaire kept tugging at their thoughts.

The Holy Spirit kept reminding them that they needed to do more than stay home and make a lot of money. The Gospel needed to be spread. And they had the tools: a desire to please Him and a craft that could be shared anywhere in the world.

They began making plans for another short-term trip. This time they wanted to take their children. That's how they came to serve at Tenwek Hospital in Kenya. They went thinking it would be short-term but ended up falling in love with the place and deciding to stay. They sold their belongings in the United States and moved to Kenya full-time.

Michael was one of the two surgeons (one of four doctors total) at the three-hundred-bed mission hospital and was soon promoted to medical superintendent. Kay served as the hospital controller. The days were busy. The needs were unrelenting.

Their children were in school five hours away. Kay could get away from time to time to visit them, but Michael wasn't that fortunate. His days were so full he barely got to see them even when they were home at the compound. Having been a surgery resident and then in private practice general surgery, missing out on family time wasn't something new. But it began to wear on them all. Michael began to run out of steam.

In addition, they were running out of money. Monthly medical school loan payments were taking their toll. When they moved to Kenya, they had no idea how it would all play out. They simply felt convinced that if the Lord wanted them to go, He'd make a way. They had cash from the sale of their house, cars, and personal belongings in Philadelphia, and their monthly income from supporters covered their living expenses. But those loan payments were slowly eating away at their personal funds. They trusted God, but this seemed like a pretty big roadblock. It began to look like they'd have to leave Kenya.

That's when they learned about MedSend.

Through a fellow doctor, they learned that MedSend would make the payments on their loans on their behalf so they could continue to serve as they followed His lead. This enabled them to continue to serve in Kenya for the next fourteen-plus years.

THE LEAST OF THESE

In the following years, Michael and Kay served at two other mission hospitals and began two ministries that focused on development work.

They saw the needs on the streets. People were hungry, eating from garbage dumps and begging. Prostitution and glue-sniffing were rampant. Michael and Kay wanted to do something. They wanted to help in a way that recognized the humanity of people in the slums. The situation was rough, but they knew the love of Christ could make a difference.

They began visiting the slums and handing out food.

As Michael says, "It's hard to preach to a hungry man."

They offered the ministry of touch—physically touching people as they offered basic medical care. Medical students from local universities joined them in their outreach, and they always tried to involve local churches.

They saw an opportunity to serve and followed the Holy Spirit's lead.

Millions of children in Kenya were made orphans by the HIV/AIDS epidemic. Between those living on the streets and those in orphanages, there were so many who had never known a home or the love of Christ. Michael and his team began holding clinics at the orphanages and providing basic care. If a child needed surgery or more involved care, they would take them to the hospital and pay for their treatment.

In addition to medical care, they were able to facilitate providing food, education, and in-country adoption services for orphans.

For a child who had never known a home or a family to be matched with a family, it was life-changing. It was a tangible, practical answer to the question, "Does God really love me?" Yes. And this is how He's provided for you—a family, a cow, a place to belong.

They saw in real ways how changing a society and cultural norms starts with the children.

They were able to help build self-sustainable sources of food and water for rural populations, and their supporters helped fund the building of a full primary school and pay for secondary and college education for orphans.

None of these development projects were things Michael had in mind when he went to Kenya as a surgeon. But God opened their eyes to the need, and God enabled them to meet it in significant ways. None of that would have happened if he'd gone home after the first four years.

When Michael and Kay eventually returned to the United States in 2010 due to health needs of their own, it wasn't to retire. They quickly began serving the least of these in their local community. They began visiting homeless shelters offering basic medical care. They would take shelter residents' blood pressure and help them get medications. They saw a need and began to do what they could to meet it.

Several months later, a local church offered a building. Soon they had donors willing to help convert the building into a medical center. After some false starts and disappointments, a contractor came forward and offered to renovate the entire building—for free. Again, God confirmed to them that He has the resources and, through the obedience of His people, the work gets done.

INSIGHT, WISDOM, AND TAKEAWAYS

Never underestimate what God can do with your faithfulness. Michael and Kay initially planned to simply send money. But by physically going, and then involving many supporters who did send money, the impact was multiplied.

They didn't personally have the money to fund all the projects they were able to do in Kenya. They wouldn't personally have been able to pay for medical care over and over again. They wouldn't personally have been able to pay for dozens of trucks of grain to go to rural Kenya. They wouldn't personally have been able to feed thousands of people, build wells, build schools. Those weren't things they could do themselves, but God did it through the faithfulness and combined efforts of God's people.

So dream big. Imagine what God can do.

Be available, willing, and obedient. Then let God figure out the details.

CHAPTER 13

STEPHEN AND JOY YOON

SOMETHING IMPOSSIBLE

I n fourth grade, Stephen Yoon got a zero on a math test. You might not think that's a big deal. What's one test?

But in South Korea, if you don't excel in academics, you have one other option: be pushed toward an athletic track—beginning as early as elementary school.

What some might consider a minor disappointing performance turned out to be a life-changing factor for Stephen. His mom decided an athletic path was more realistic for her son and signed him up for swimming. She enrolled him in a physical education middle school and physical education high school. At the time, Korea was producing a number of Olympic swimmers, and Stephen was eventually scouted for that program.

In high school, Stephen was introduced to an organization that focused on helping athletes know Christ, and he became a Christian. During a weekend retreat, Stephen watched the speaker onstage with rapt attention. He leaned in as the student athletes were asked to respond to this invitation:

"If God is asking you to go to a certain country and serve for Him, will you go?"

At the time Stephen assumed everyone was feeling what he was feeling. After all, if God asked you to do something, why wouldn't you do it? No question. But to his surprise, he was one of only a handful of people who accepted the challenge. The die was cast. That night he committed his life to serving God wherever He might ask him to go.

When it came time for college, Stephen still didn't worry too much about academics. He had an athletic scholarship to pursue a degree in physical education and plans to become a swimming coach. In his junior year, at a time of prayer, he felt God was challenging him to do *something impossible*.

Because he was a high-level athlete, he never really had to study. The government approved padding his grades so that he could continue to compete.

His first impossible thought was, *Maybe I could go to grad school or get my doctorate and become a professor. Something academic.*

But he didn't have peace in his heart.

It's almost as if God smiled and said, "That's not impossible. You could actually do that."

Then he began to think of medicine and what serving God with those skills might look like. That *definitely* sounded impossible.

So at the age of twenty-three, Stephen Yoon prayed, "Lord, if You really want me to experience the God who makes the impossible possible . . . here is my life. If I can serve You through healthcare ministry, I will."

He began to pray about where God would ask him to serve. He knew that for it to be impossible, it needed to be a place that pushed him out of his comfort zone.

Growing up in South Korea, he knew the foremost enemy was not North Korea but Japan. Because of past wars and oppression, there was a vast divide between Koreans and Japanese. But God challenged Stephen to love people whom he disliked or could not accept, even the Japanese. Could he embrace the people he had been taught to hate the most?

And then Stephen learned about the concept of the 10/40 Window. Named after the area between 10° and 40° North latitude, this rectangular area represents places in the world where the gospel is the least accepted. But while the gospel isn't always welcomed there, medical professionals *are*, and they are able to minister in these countries where regular pastors cannot.

Stephen set his heart toward one of those countries—most likely an Islamic or communist nation.

With very little grasp of English, Stephen moved to the United States to begin the impossible task of gaining medical training. After a year and a half of English classes, he enrolled as a freshman biology major at a small college outside Chicago. Without any science or math prerequisites on his record, Stephen started college all over again.

It was time to do the impossible.

JOY, MEET STEPHEN

"Joy, there's one Korean on campus. You have to meet him."

Joy's sister graduated from the college Joy would attend one semester before Joy started. She knew how challenging the transition to college might be and thought a friendly Korean face would mean a whole lot. Joy had lived most of her childhood in South Korea with her professor parents. She was an American citizen, but the small college campus in a cornfield in Illinois was a long way from home and a long way from anything familiar.

As God would plan things, Joy ended up in the same freshman biology class as Stephen. They bonded over shared experiences and ended up studying together and driving to Chicago for good Korean food.

As a child growing up, Joy had no intention of following in her parents' footsteps or even returning to Korea. She wanted to find a small town in the United States and put down roots. She wanted to finally belong somewhere. No more being from one place but living in another and not really claiming rights to either. No more confusion about her identity.

But God had other plans.

At one conference when Joy was fifteen years old, she heard very clearly from God:

I want you to go. And the call was very specific: *I want you to go to North Korea.*

Finally, unexplainably, Joy felt the peace and assurance that her teenage heart had been longing for. It didn't come from roots in a small town in the United States. It came from a deep understanding that God had a plan for her life, and He'd had it all along. Perhaps this is why He allowed her to grow up as a confused third-culture kid in South Korea. Perhaps her childhood had uniquely positioned her to serve God in North Korea.

But still . . . it was North Korea, one of the least accessible places on earth. God must have a sense of humor *and* a desire to do something impossible.

As her friendship with Stephen blossomed, they spent time praying about whether their callings were compatible.

Joy was clear. "God has called me to North Korea. I'm not saying that I'm unwilling to serve in other countries, but I have an assurance from God that someday it will be there. If you're not willing to end up there someday, I don't think there's a future for our relationship."

North Korea was not a country Stephen had ever considered. All his life he'd been taught that North Koreans were horrible, scary, even evil. In elementary school, North Koreans were depicted in their textbooks drawn with horns and tails. Stephen could not fathom North Korea as a place of service. It was a place Koreans could not go. They would never even think about it. Why would they? It was like going to the moon—impossible.

When Joy asked, "Would you be willing to go to North Korea with me?"

Of course, he said yes. He trusted that his good God, who always gives good things, would never, ever let that happen. He said yes, trusting that God would never send them there.

He was wrong.

After college, both Stephen and Joy were accepted to chiropractic college in Chicago, but neither of them had peace about it. Stephen felt a calling into ministry instead of graduate school right away, and Joy was unsure about pursuing the medical field.

Through a connection with Stephen's former youth pastor, they ended up moving to Los Angeles to work in youth ministry and music at a small Korean-American congregation. They served there for the next seven years and eventually began graduate studies—Stephen in chiropractic medicine and Joy in biology.

All the while, God was preparing their hearts through short-term trips to China and connections with other cross-cultural workers.

During this time, Stephen received a scholarship to attend a conference on North Korea. There he heard about and met foreign Christians living in North Korea, even raising their children there. It was shocking.

Though that conference was only a weekend long, it changed Stephen's life forever. He came home saying, "Joy, I think God is calling us to North Korea!"

Joy's response was simple, "Yes, I know. I've been praying for that for seven years now!"

They began to make concrete plans to go to North Korea. They attended another conference where their hearts were stirred to simply be obedient and go. Go now, and let God provide the means.

The next year was a whirlwind of preparation. They finished medical training and graduate school, applied to and were accepted by a sending organization, co-led another short-term trip to China, sold or gave away all their belongings, and watched as God amazingly provided the necessary financial support.

Stephen was invited to start teaching and treating patients through chiropractic medicine at a traditional Korean medicine hospital, and fifteen years after Joy had felt the initial call, they and their two small children moved to live in North Korea.

DON'T RELY ON YOUR SKILLS

On the day Stephen and Joy were to cross the border into North Korea for the first time, Stephen was sick. Or he wanted to say he was sick—sick and could not go. He was nervous, scared. All he could see was the childhood image of North Koreans with horns and tails. He imagined they would swallow him if he did something wrong.

On that day their assigned escort was late. They waited at the border for over two hours, anxious, freezing cold, and hungry from not having eaten lunch. When their minder finally approached, Joy said, "Wow, he's so handsome."

Something inside Stephen shifted. *Oh. He is a good-looking man. He's a regular person. Just like us. North Koreans are people just like us.*

During the hour's drive from the border into town, the minder asked questions, trying to make conversation. All Stephen could say was "Yes" or "No" as he reminded himself: *Calm down, relax. He's just making conversation.*

Stephen was nervous, but for the first time in his life, he was able to break through the propaganda of his childhood and recognize the truth: North Koreans were people whom God loves.

And God wasn't done stretching and challenging Stephen and Joy. They had prayed about this move and were convinced that God was calling them to go. They had even reconciled that if they had to die there to follow God's call, they would do it. But even with that kind of faith, Stephen confesses that he never thought God was alive in North Korea. Every bit of news or information about North Korea was not of God. It's all what the enemy and darkness have done to that nation.

That all changed when Stephen began treating patients.

When he first arrived at the hospital, his predecessor took Stephen aside to a private room.

They prayed together, and then the older man said, "Today you are going to rely upon God. You cannot rely upon your medical knowledge or your skills here."

In the beginning, all his patients were old with very difficult chronic issues.

He found himself saying again and again, "I'm sorry. You came too late. I cannot help you. You need surgery, and I can't do that."

Knowing they could not receive surgery in the country, he had to simply give them basic treatment and send them home. Stephen was disappointed. Why had God sent him here if he wasn't going to be of any use?

But then, amazingly, his patients began to be healed. As a chiropractor, his treatment was all manual. He had to adjust people by physically touching their bodies. And as he laid hands on them in treatment and silently prayed over them, they began to see miraculous results.

A grandmother who hadn't been able to move her arm for years suddenly could. A patient who had been brought in by piggyback because he was completely disabled by pain got up and walked out of the treatment room.

Stephen knew it wasn't because of the basic treatments he was giving—his patients' conditions were so severe. There was no explanation other than that God was healing them one by one. And Stephen received the message loud and clear: God is alive and well here.

He is the one who heals.

He is the one changing impossible to possible.

COUNTRY-CHANGING MEDICAL CARE

Word of these hundreds of miraculous healings spread. More and more difficult patients came in for treatment. In 2012, a grandmother brought in her four-year-old granddaughter with severe spastic quadriplegia. She had cerebral palsy and could not even move a finger. Her jaw was locked open. The grandmother had kept her alive by pre-chewing food and transferring it to the little girl's mouth so she could swallow it.

As Stephen held this little girl, his heart broke, and he asked a question many have asked before:

Why, God? Why should this beautiful child be born here in North Korea with this horrible condition?

He wept over her. He had never treated kids with cerebral palsy, but he tried his best with all the knowledge and skills and prayer he could offer.

And then he started asking questions. "Why is this the first CP patient I've seen in all these years? Are there not more kids like this?"

The answer he received from North Korean doctors was not comforting. "Actually, when a child like this is born, we tell parents not to let them suffer too long. Let them die quickly and in peace."

From that time on, Stephen dropped everything else. He would do whatever it took to help people see the value in all lives—even those severely disabled.

At the time, since there was no medical training or therapy to treat children with developmental disabilities like cerebral palsy or autism in North Korea, he traveled to South Korea to learn pediatric rehabilitation.

After a few years, Stephen was invited to move from the northern province to the capital city of Pyongyang to teach rehabilitation medicine at North Korea's top medical school. More and more people who'd been hidden away in their homes started coming out, seeking treatment.

One came to them a quadriplegic. She received treatment for a whole year. She was admitted, received surgeries and therapies, and she became the first CP quadriplegic patient to walk out of the hospital on her own power.

Again, the good news spread. The North Korean broadcasting company even did a documentary on her story. In 2014 Kim Jong Un himself heard the report, and the North Korean Ministry of Public Health eventually agreed to establish pediatric rehabilitation centers in all ten provincial hospitals in the country.

As the programs grew, Stephen and Joy never forgot that first little four-year-old girl. Sadly, because it took time to raise the support needed to build a hospital and get the expertise needed to treat children like her, her family gave up hope, and she passed away. But her life planted a seed for a treatment program for the entire nation. Because of her, all the children of North Korea would have opportunities to grow and develop to their fullest potential. It's no mistake that her name was Bok Shin, literally translated as "Blessing."

While Stephen was focused on the medical aspect of treatment, Joy could not ignore the educational effects. Most of the kids seeking rehab treatment were not going to school because of their developmental disabilities. There were no programs available for them.

In the early years living in the northern province, Joy had been busy homeschooling their children, but with the move to Pyongyang came the opportunity to enroll the children in a school for diplomats' children. Now available during the days, Joy began to go with Stephen to the hospital and watch the kids receive treatment. Many of these children had never learned how to read or write even as teenagers. It wasn't because they weren't smart. They simply had never had the opportunity to go to school or really even leave their homes.

Joy began to advocate for their education.

As an American, she knew she had to tread lightly. Americans are usually thought of as archenemies to North Koreans. Thankfully, a Korean-Chinese teammate could help. She had an acceptable heritage, and Joy had training in education. Together they began to teach these children. Joy would make all the preparations and create all the lesson plans and then show her teammate how to implement them. They made a good team.

Soon Joy was asked to teach the children English and help them overcome their speech impediments in speaking. When Joy's Korean-Chinese teammate got married and left to join her husband, Joy took over the whole program. She found herself with the great privilege of teaching North Korean children in their own language how to read and write their own language. That they would trust her was something significant—a huge honor.

As she continued to work with these children, she realized that in addition to the developmental disabilities, they also had learning challenges. Joy went back to school online and earned her certification in special education and educational therapy. And during a visit back to the United States, she trained in the neurodevelopmental approach so she could provide a therapeutic approach to education that would help children with disabilities and autism achieve their best potential.

It's not something either of them could have envisioned as college students in Illinois, but they are grateful for the winding road God has let them down. They receive so much joy from seeing children improve and gain function and skills. It's just another way God has provided for them to love people. To witness dramatic transformations in the lives of their patients and changing perspectives from their colleagues is a precious gift.

INSIGHT, WISDOM, AND TAKEAWAYS

"God is rarely early, but He's never late," Stephen says.

We tend to want to know things ahead of time. We want our lives planned. We want to know what and how and when God is going to do things. But that wouldn't require faith. God wants us to grow our faith in Him. Trust God each step of the way. He will always come through on time. It's usually just in the nick of time because God wants to see you grow in a deeper relationship with Him.

Many cross-cultural humanitarian workers approach their service as if they are bringing something—food or medicine—to a country that needs their help. Stephen and Joy have found that the real work has been done in their own hearts. North Korea is the place they have learned to walk intimately with God. They know they would not last long in this challenging location if their focus was only on meeting others' physical and medical needs. In this place, they must trust God every day—in that way they receive more than they give. That is the greatest gift of serving.

And if the situation seems impossible, trust God and rest in His love. Nothing is impossible for Him.

CHAPTER 14

TOM AND LIBBY LITTLE

STAY

I n 1978 Tom and Libby Little and their two young daughters were living in Herat, Afghanistan, near the border of Iran. Tom was helping finish the construction of a ten-bed ophthalmology hospital, the only medical facility in the western part of the country. He wasn't trained in construction, but he did have experience with eyes and medical care—and he was one of the few people willing to be there.

There had been a political coup (one of many to come), and most foreigners had left the country. But not Tom and Libby. They stuck around, willing to do what they could. Medical care in this western area was lacking. It was simply too difficult for people to leave their farms and families and travel all the way to the capital city of Kabul for eye care. The plan was to get the hospital up and running, train some local people in basic eye care, and then have a doctor come out from Kabul, over five hundred miles to the east.

Tom and Libby knew the political situation was tenuous, but they had only been in the country about a year, and they were optimistic. Their focus was on accomplishing the task at hand. They had no idea what was to come. Sometimes God spares you the details because He knows you aren't ready. They were simply trying to serve where there was a need. Tom focused on the eye hospital, and Libby focused on their daughters. She met their neighbors and got settled into their new surroundings.

Just six months later, there was another coup and a bloody revolution. This time it was the Soviets invading Afghanistan. And it was right through Herat, their backyard. By that time, Tom and Libby were one of only a few Western families still in the area. Their mission agency urged them to evacuate the country, but Tom resisted. He felt like they were really supposed to stay and get the hospital open.

And so they did. They stayed in that dry, dusty village, trusting God with whatever was to come.

They saw the panic and fear in their neighbor's eyes as the Soviets poured over the border.

They lost an opportunity to take a chartered plane out. They lost the opportunity to be part of a convoy of a few foreigners leaving the area. And then Tom and Libby Little lost their names.

As their neighbors watched the chartered plane and the convoy of tanks and armored vehicles leave, they saw the Littles stay.

It must have been a marking moment. Because from then on, Tom and Libby were no longer called *Mr. Tom* and *Mr. Tom's Half*. They became known as *The People Who Stayed with Us*.

Tom and Libby didn't stay because it was exciting. It wasn't a sense of adventure or duty. They didn't even know if they could make a difference in this wartime environment. In fact, talking to Libby four decades later, it's clear she wanted to leave every single day. But the phenomenal reaction of their neighbors to their staying through the most difficult experiences of their lives could not be ignored.

The tense political situation continued to devolve. Tom and Libby were aware of the upheaval but somewhat removed from the death and bloody chaos. That all changed one night when the local mobs rose up against the Soviets and any Soviet advisers and entered their city on a killing rampage.

The Littles spent that night of terror hiding in an underground kitchen in their backyard with their two young daughters. It seemed as if all hell had broken loose around them as the street in front of their mud house was continuously strafed with bullets.

The next morning a neighbor came over the five-and-a-half-foot walls around their home with fresh bread and warm, sweet milk from their cows. It was still too dangerous to go out on the street, so the neighbors fed them and, as Tom and Libby would later find out, had also saved their lives.

On that most terrifying night, one local man made his way to their door. Libby had befriended his daughter and her baby months earlier, and this man remembered that kindness. Planting himself firmly in the doorway, he stayed in front of their gate all night as the violent, angry mob swept through town looking for Soviet advisers.

As the mob gathered in front of their door, he said, "These are people of the book. Pass on by!"

All night long, he stood—an imperfect protector, undaunted and unwavering.

Early in the morning, thoroughly shaken by the experiences of the night, they were surprised to find this man still at their door, exhausted but alive.

"Why are you here?" they asked.

"I told the mobs to pass you by," he said. "Because you stayed with us. You are one of us."

And that's when Libby says she felt like God told her: "You're going to be here for a while, so just get used to it."

Even as I spoke with Libby, I thought about what it must have been like to be in Afghanistan in the late 1970s and stay for over thirty years. At the time of this writing, this beleaguered country has been part of our consciousness for nearly twenty years, but it's always had a tumultuous history.

Tom and Libby were there during the first coup, there when the Soviets invaded, there when the Soviets withdrew. They witnessed the aftermath of a civil war. They were there for the formation of Al Qaeda. They were there during the rise of the Taliban. They were there when the US Armed Forces arrived.

And yet, through it all, they stayed.

I asked Libby what that was like. It's hard to even fathom, let alone answer.

Libby says, "I could tell you the physical highlights of what happened, but what was happening *in us* was much more significant. Yes, there was a war *outside* for thirty years, but there was also this great war and struggle inside. It wasn't so much that God called us to *do* something in Afghanistan, but that He called us to *stay*."

That word *stay* would become the most significant word in Tom and Libby's lives.

WHY AFGHANISTAN?

Like some of the other medical professionals you're reading about in this book, Tom and Libby didn't have strong aspirations to be missionaries. Their initial call was shaky at best. But somehow, God has a way of arranging circumstances to get people where He wants them to be.

As newlyweds, Tom and Libby had an interest in ministry, a bit of an adventurous streak, and a desire to chart their own course. They also had family pressures. Tom's father was convinced that Tom should study as an optometrist and take over the family eye care practice.

There was just one problem with this plan: Tom didn't want that life. But neither did he want to hurt his father whom he loved very much.

So when the call of God came to go overseas, it sounded a lot like, "Let's escape." Their way of escape came through an acquaintance in Kabul, Afghanistan.

In the late 1970s, Kabul was a bottleneck along a "hippie trail" around the Middle East—India, Nepal, and Afghanistan. Their acquaintance asked them to run a halfway house for hippie drug addicts who were passing through. Tom and Libby liked the idea of inviting troubled peers into a home and doing Bible studies and helping them get back on their feet. They figured they could go for a year or two—it would buy them some time with Tom's father—and they could figure it out after that.

After a couple months of training, having never even smoked so much as a cigarette themselves, they went from a seminary in the United States to working with drug addicts in Afghanistan—all to avoid Tom's father.

That was the summer of 1977, and at the time, things were relatively politically stable. The American embassy was functioning, and there were other foreigners in the city. There was also a huge mass of drug addicts in "drug hotels" and in great distress. So Tom and Libby, along with some other helpers, ran a house for up to twenty men, women, and sometimes even their children. They were severely addicted, but they had questions and were open to talking about the Bible. And it didn't hurt that there was food involved. Several times a week, Tom would make a trip to these hippie hotels and gather people to come back for a pancake meal at their house. That went on for a year—until the first political coup.

Soon the hippie house had to close. The government cracked down, and the Soviet influence was growing. Tom was already volunteering at one mission in Afghanistan, which was a blind school eye hospital. Because he had a background in eye care from working with his father, he was in demand.

"Please set up an optical shop."

"We want to grind our own lenses."

"Would you teach refraction to our doctors?"

Tom trained as many as he could before things got too tense to continue. Then he and Libby had a choice. They could go to Herat and help build the eye hospital there. Faced with the choice of going home or going to Herat, they chose Herat, having no idea of all that was to come.

And Tom's father? He simply could not believe that his son was indeed doing eye care—all the way on the other side of the world.

MEDICINE IN A WAR ZONE

After that horrible night of terror in Herat, it was only a matter of time before all foreigners were completely forced out of the outlying areas of the country. Tom had succeeded in helping open the hospital, only to have it taken over by the Soviets. What the quality of the eye care looked like depended on the day and who was in power as the hospital changed hands.

Eventually, the Littles were forced back to Kabul. When the time came, it was sudden and immediate: "Leave now, with nothing but yourselves."

They left everything behind—photo albums, living supplies, and the kind neighbors who had accepted them as their own.

Back in Kabul, with all foreigners leaving the country, Libby naturally thought they would be on the next flight out. This little adventure had come to an end. It was time to go back to America. But Tom was asked to be the director of the eye clinic in Kabul . . . because everybody else was leaving.

Even though everyone else was leaving, Tom and Libby kept hearing that word: *Stay*.

So they did. They could not escape the call to stay.

Life went on, and in 1982, Tom and Libby went back to America so she could deliver her third daughter. They soon began getting telegrams.

"When are you coming back?"

"Please come back."

"We need you here."

Libby was comfortable in her little home in upstate New York. Not surprisingly, they were working with Afghan refugees.

We're doing our part here, she thought.

But as they wrestled with what to do with the messages coming from Afghanistan, it was as if God was saying, "There are a lot of people here that can work with refugees. I want you back in Afghanistan."

So they went back, this time with three young daughters . . . and this time into a fully Soviet-occupied country.

Upon their arrival back in the country, they discovered that the hospital in Kabul had been bombed and taken over by various groups fighting the Soviets. They also discovered that Tom had some God-given capacity that not everyone else did. When things fell apart, he could see ways to put them back together again. He seemed custom-made by God to be relaxed in very tense and dangerous situations.

Tom threw himself into doing whatever was needed. He called himself a gopher as he became the medical supplies person going out with a backpack and a big duffel bag seeking raw materials. Eye drops, medicines, new hospital equipment—all kinds of things that it takes to run a hospital in an active war zone. At this time, there was no electricity in the city, so he found a way to get small, portable solar panels from India. Tom was the one who did all the running back and forth and crossing front lines.

When the hospital was bombed, there were four front lines in the city fighting the Soviets. There were many eye injuries from bullets, rockets, landmines, and grenades, and the Red Cross workers would often call on Tom for help. He would get on his bike and go get one of the eye doctors and deliver him to the Red Cross on the back of his bike. Once the surgery was done, Tom would bike him back before making his way home to Libby and the girls. Or after a rocket attack, he would go out and simply help pick up bodies. Awful things were happening, and there was no escaping it.

Remarkably, even under these difficult circumstances, God enabled Tom and others to open four clinics on the four front lines around Kabul staffed with whatever eye doctor was trained in that area.

In the late 1980s, the Soviets withdrew from the country, but it did not result in peace. Stockpiles of ammunition fell into the hands of Afghan warlords, and they started fighting with each other in a bloody civil war. The bombing was near constant. The Littles counted a hundred bombs a day, until finally they just stopped counting.

The living room of their sandbagged, windowless home became a triage center for the injured. The clinics were barely able to be open, but the need was great. The doctors wouldn't come out of hiding because they'd be taken to the front lines. Everybody was scared.

During the civil war of the early 1990s, Libby says she wanted to leave every day. And who could blame her? But then she would join Tom on his rounds. They would sneak up to the hospital that they had regained. It was a bombed-out makeshift mess, and only a few rooms could be used. As they made their rounds, they saw that it was down to a handful of people running an eye hospital in a war zone. If they left, who would help these doctors?

Again, they thought of their neighbors. How could they tell their neighbors they had to leave? That it was too dangerous for their daughters? How could they explain the necessity of leaving to a neighbor with ten children who had no option to leave?

So again, they stayed.

Then in the mid-1990s, the Taliban took over. Surprisingly, during the Taliban era, they were able to expand medical care to some of the remote areas of the country. As long as they conducted a few clinics in the Taliban areas, they were allowed to go to remote, underserved areas, fixing eyes and planting seeds.

In addition to providing acute medical care, Tom had a vision for a training program. Tom and a team of medical professionals would go to a remote area where there was very little medical care of any kind and no eye care.

Tom's team would ask the leader of that area, "Who's your smartest kid?"

They would offer to take him for two years to Kabul, pay his expenses, and provide housing while he went through a training program. At the end of the two years, he'd go back to his village—fully trained and ready to give sight to the blind.

In the early 2000s, the US Armed Forces invaded, the Taliban was ousted, and everything changed again. Outreach efforts to remote areas were more restricted, difficult, and dangerous, but amazingly, women were now able to take their training courses.

Tom also began work on a new clinic specifically set up for the Hazara people, one of the most discriminated against ethnic minority groups in the country. The Hazara have long faced violence and mistreatment, and Tom felt there should be a clinic in the area of the city where they were all huddled together in danger. He got creative, taking three discarded Soviet containers, cutting holes for windows and doors, and turning them into a clinic complete with room for surgeries.

Because of Tom's resourcefulness, the village wouldn't have to wait for a medical team to come along every four or five years—they had one of their own trained and ready to help.

GOD CREATES THE IMPACT

Through all these chaotic years, Libby is clear to point out that they were not evangelists. They were doing very practical things. Most of the time, they, like their Afghan neighbors, were simply trying to survive in a war zone. They had to question the impact of their presence there. Sure, they were helping with medical needs, but were they making any kind of impact for the kingdom?

Yet even as she struggled to stay, God reminded Libby of His presence and His work. In Herat, that gentle reminder came through a visit from a woman named Rosemary.

Rosemary was a missionary nurse who lived and worked in Pakistan and Afghanistan. The Littles didn't have a lot of extras—having guests was rather a hardship in those days—but they welcomed her to stay in their home as they prepared for Christmas.

There weren't any trees to serve as a Christmas tree, but they had a little nativity set, and they'd made a few decorations. And Rosemary had brought a flannelgraph set.

Libby's girls were quite taken with Rosemary and her stories, so she suggested they invite a couple of their little friends over. They'd have a birthday party for Jesus, complete with a flannelgraph story. It wasn't an outreach or something they planned for the neighborhood. It was simply a holiday diversion for the girls and their friends.

Those two or three friends told their mothers. The mothers told their neighbors. And within minutes that morning, their small "kids' birthday party for Jesus" turned into an event. Before Libby knew what was happening, her tiny living room in the mud house was packed with women, children, and crying babies.

Libby had never seen so many people together at one time in Herat. She was worried about being a good host; she only had six teacups after all. But the women weren't bothered. "Oh, we'll just pass them around," they said.

So Libby made tea, and Rosemary pulled out her flannelgraph and started to tell the story of Jesus, beginning at creation. The women were captivated. They wept.

They said, "We've never heard this before. I left my mother back at the house with the baby. I want to go get her. Can you tell it again?"

Throughout the day, as the women came and went, Rosemary repeated the good news, and Libby made pot after pot of tea.

And through the low, open windows, they kept hearing, "Is this the right house? Is this the home of the people who stayed?"

That evening, when Tom arrived home from the hospital and heard what had happened, he was concerned. He knew they weren't supposed to be proselytizing, and he didn't want to jeopardize their position in the community or their ability to continue working on the hospital.

"We didn't do it on purpose!" Libby said. "It just happened. They just kept coming. There was nothing we could do about it."

The words were hardly out of her mouth when they were startled by an awful, angry banging on their door. The village men were outside, and they were upset.

"You need to learn, if there's anything important to say, you must tell the men first," they said. "Your wife has been telling our women the news and not us, and we are insulted. We want to hear it too. You are the ones who stayed with us, and if you have something to say, we want to hear it."

Libby, Rosemary, and the girls were hanging back, partially hiding behind the door, when the men demanded to come in. As Tom explained that his language skills were still rudimentary, Rosemary presented herself in an appropriate way and said she'd tell the story to the men if they'd allow her.

Once again, Rosemary proceeded to tell the good news about Jesus, from beginning to end. This time to a group of Muslim men.

Many of those men were killed shortly after that in the night of terror as they defended the farmers and the city. Who can say what impact this night had in the lives of these men? In God's way, in His timing, seeds of truth were planted.

Throughout the years, the Lord continued to give Libby small glimpses of the ways He was working through her in the awful, chaotic circumstances.

During the years of heavy bombing in Kabul, the main floor of their house was bombed, so they lived in the basement. Often neighbor women and children would sneak over to share the relative safety of the basement as the rockets fell. You might think that this would be a good time to evangelize and proclaim the gospel. But Libby says you don't think that way when you're being bombed. You are as scared as everybody else, and you're holding your children just like they're holding theirs. You are all on the same level. But even if you aren't aware of it, God's Spirit is always on the move.

The seeds you may not even know you're planting during those trying times often yield the most beautiful fruits. Five years after one of these harrowing times, a woman came back to Libby and asked if she remembered her.

"I was in your basement," she said. "You were alone with your girls."

Libby told her, "I'm sorry, I don't remember you."

And thinking back, she thought, *There were a lot of people in my basement during that time. And yes, I was often alone. Tom was usually out at the hospitals with patients or picking up dead bodies and working at the Red Cross Emergency Center.*

"You just kept saying, 'Jesus.' That's all you said. You weren't saying it loudly or for anyone else to hear. You were just whispering it in your daughters' ears as you held them. And every time I heard the name of Jesus come out of your mouth, I felt a warmth come through my whole body. As I felt that warmth come over me, I could not wait to get out of Afghanistan to find someone who would tell me about this Jesus."

And where had this woman ended up? She traveled as a refugee to Australia . . . where she was met by a group of Christians from a church who told her all about Jesus.

As she recounted this story in her soft-spoken voice, Libby said people often have to *see* the gospel before they can hear it. It's God who warms people's hearts. We can have our strategies and our methods and our goals and all the words, but in the end, it's the still, small voice of God that changes people's hearts.

We don't know how He does it, but we're confident that He does. And that confidence is what carried her through all those difficult years.

JOY AND SACRIFICE

With all the trauma and upheaval of their years in Afghanistan, it was their daughters that Libby worried about most. How was this affecting them—all the danger, the scary nights, and staying in a dugout kitchen in the backyard, and dealing with all those traumatic injuries in their living room turned triage center.

What kind of a childhood was that?

And their education—their daughters went away to boarding school in Northern India because there weren't good options available for them in Kabul. Sending them away was the best option at the time, but as you might imagine, a difficult choice for a mother to make. It was hard for Tom and Libby to have them be so far away and miss out on that formative time in their girls' lives. And it was rough for the daughters.

This was before the internet made communication easy. That meant they had to deal with not hearing from their parents for a month at a time waiting for handwritten letters to arrive. In those times, they would read in the Indian newspapers about the slaughter in Afghanistan. But they made it, and as the girls grew up, they still thought of Afghanistan as their home. Even in the early 2000s under the Taliban and the strict regulations around women, they still wanted to come back to Kabul for their gap year between high school and college.

Libby says she wishes she could have kept them from all that, and she'll always cry over those years of not being with them in ordinary ways, but her daughters have grown into amazing people, and even now, they're doing wonderful things with their lives.

When it came time to make plans for Tom and Libby to celebrate their fortieth wedding anniversary in 2010, Libby had two requests: she wanted to go home to America, and she wanted to be with her three now-adult daughters—all of them together under one roof for a week.

They gathered in Upstate New York in a cabin in the Adirondacks in July 2010. They spent a glorious week together—enjoying the peace of the mountains and soaking in their time together.

It was an absolute gift from God and everything Libby hoped it would be.

At the end of their week together, on July 18, their anniversary day, Tom flew back to Kabul while Libby stayed behind in New York. Their first grandchild was due in another month, and nothing could pull her away before she held that new baby in her arms. She planned to help her daughter get settled and speak at churches about the work in Afghanistan. Tom would go back to lead an outreach team to a remote part of the country.

It was going to be a challenging trip squeezed into a short window of time and in a very dangerous place. The place they were headed was the Nuristan province. It was a remote valley hanging between rocky mountains that stretched to the sky. Tom and a team of seven other foreign aid workers, along with two Afghan guides, would have to cross over a nearly 17,000-foot mountain pass to get to the village and deliver the medical supplies.

Tom and the team drove from Kabul for two days up into the northern area of the country, then trekked on foot for two days, carrying the needed equipment on donkeys and in backpacks. Tom carried a satellite phone and was able to contact Libby every day. He would call and give her updates, sharing their progress on the trek there, the stories of people they were helping, and anything else significant that she had to relay by email to their contacts in Kabul or supporters in the United States.

But on August 5, she didn't hear anything—no call in the morning and no call in the afternoon. Libby says only twice in her life has she felt that she's heard the voice of God, but she clearly heard that day:

This is going to be very hard. Stay close to Me.

After a sleepless night of praying and weeping, the next morning Libby learned that the group had been ambushed and murdered by the Taliban on their way back over the mountains.

Thirty-three years after setting foot on Afghanistan soil, Tom Little's mission was finished.

In a devastated fog, Libby and her daughters scrambled to renew visas and book tickets to fly back to Kabul. The bodies of the other members of the team were transported back to their home countries, but Libby and her daughters felt strongly that Tom should be buried in Kabul. The family of Dan Terry, the other senior man on the team, felt the same, and so the two men were buried side by side in Kabul. The daughters of the two men put together a small service, and it was overwhelmed with people— ordinary Afghans whose lives had been touched by Tom and Dan.

And then Libby finally got to go home. Her daughters insisted. They packed up all of Tom's memories, put Libby's clothes out in the street, and directed the US government that instead of flying their father's body home, they could fly his belongings.

So with ten boxes of Tom's things, Libby moved into the small house in Upstate New York that they had purchased back in the early eighties when they had come back to the United States for the birth of their third daughter.

All these years she had longed for this home, for a place to sink down roots in safety and calm. Now she could.

CHANGED

After Tom's death, Libby's mission organization asked if she would travel around and speak about missions.

You can almost hear the humility and laughter in her response when she thought, *Boy, am I the wrong one for this. They've got their people mixed up. It should be Tom.*

But without Libby's sacrifice, there would be no Tom.

Libby stayed when she wanted to go home.

Libby served when she wanted to hold her girls.

Libby shared when she had nothing to give.

Together, Tom and Libby Little poured themselves into Afghanistan, and although she may not see the fruit of her labors this side of heaven, their work and their sacrifice changed things.

It changed people.

It changed me.

CHAPTER 15

THE REIMAGINED MISSION

There's a reason Jesus taught in parables. Parables are stories, and stories are sticky.

They get down in our soul. They speak to us in a language of their own. They make us want to lean in, listen up, and pay attention. They often teach us something about ourselves—who we are or who we are becoming. They convict us, convince us, and compel us. They tap into something deeply human in all of us—a desire to *write our own story*—and to live it out in a way that makes a difference. That's what makes the stories you just read so captivating. You just got to witness the stories of people all around the world, serving as the hands and feet of Jesus.

But hopefully, you witnessed more than that. Hopefully, you got a new glimpse of what "missions" are.

For years missionary work looked a certain way. It was "us" going over there to serve "them." It was, "Dr. Livingstone, I presume?" It was coming back to raise support. It was evangelizing in the deepest, darkest, most remote corners of the world. I'm not knocking it—much good was done in the world.

These stories you've just read, however, show you what the future might look like. As the world continues to fall apart, and as borders get tighter and it's harder to get into the places where the need is greatest, these medical missionaries can use their trade and their talents to serve deeply human needs *and* share the love of Christ when people are at their most vulnerable.

But each one would tell you that they are nothing special. They were just doing what God called them to do. In fact, as I interviewed them to get their stories, it took a while to get them to open up, share the struggles, and admit that their story oftentimes was hard.

That said, they would never back down or quit because God gave them the story and they wanted to live it out, to see how it ended.

Which brings me to you . . .

What's your story? Do you know?

Our stories often look and feel disjointed for one big reason: we aren't clear on our mission.

You don't have to be called as a global missionary to have a mission. You don't have to sell all your goods and move halfway across the world. You don't have to take on educational debt and become a medical professional. You don't even have to leave your neighborhood.

The truth is, there are needs all around you, right now, that you have been uniquely created to address. You have the gifts. You have the talents. You have the heart.

Do you have the desire to use your God-given gifts?

My hope is that in reading these stories, you don't just close this book and say, "Well, that was nice. Those people are making a difference. But I could never do that." Rather, my hope is that as you've read these stories, you've sensed a stirring in your own heart.

My prayer is that the God who called Cathy and Bubba Hoelzer to the toughest places on earth, Katherine Welch to the seedy streets of Bangkok, Carol Spears to the UAE to demonstrate the love of Jesus without saying his name, John Cropsey to Rwanda to start an ophthalmology residency program, Boaz Niyinyumva to flee genocide and listen to that still, small voice, Belyse Arakaza to watch God confuse the science, Faith Lelei to examine if someone had to have white skin to serve as a missionary, Geoffrey Moses to a place with some of the worst healthcare statistics in the world, Perry Jansen to battle HIV/AIDS on the front lines, Michael Johnson to dream big for the underserved in Kenya, Stephen and Joy Yoon to go to one of the most misunderstood places in the world and simply share the love of Jesus, Tom Little to give his life after decades of service, and Libby Little to stay obedient until she finally got to go home, and even me to MedSend is calling you right now.

Where is He calling you? To discover *your* mission. And to *write your story*.

A NEW MISSION

To help you find your mission, let me share a little bit of how I came to mine.

There's a reason you read Tom and Libby Little's story last. That's because it is interwoven with my story. You may remember from chapter one that right around the time I got connected to MedSend, I met Tom and Libby in person and heard their compelling story.

At the time I was bivocational—pastoring a church in Connecticut while also getting my bearings at MedSend from my tiny closet office. I generally kept the two parts of my story separate.

That is, until I got the email from Tom saying he and a team were going back over the mountains in Afghanistan to reach a remote village and deliver training and supplies. He knew it would be dangerous. The Taliban were hot and heavy in the region, and even the US military was pulling back from their remote bases in the area. But Tom was compelled to go.

His email simply asked for prayer. For the first time, I let my work as a pastor and my work at MedSend intersect.

The next Sunday morning, from the pulpit at Black Rock Church in Stamford, Connecticut, I shared Tom's request for prayer with the congregation. I prayed over Tom and asked them to please do the same. The following week, I got an email from Libby saying she was concerned, she hadn't heard from Tom, and again the request was simple:

"Would you please pray?"

Finally, we got the terrible, hard-to-understand news. Tom and the team had been ambushed and killed.

Thirty-three years of faithful service had ended in a senseless (at least to me) tragedy.

Ambushed by the Taliban, Tom and his team had been gunned down on a steep mountain peak in the middle of a war zone, trying to share compassionate love and, in their own way, bless a hurting world.

I was heartbroken. Angry. Confused.

How could this be? Why would God allow this tragedy to happen to Christians who had committed their entire lives to following him in the hardest of places? MedSend had 150 people in seventy-five countries around the world. How was it that the only people I had met and gotten to know had been martyred?

Whole books have been written on why God doesn't intervene in these situations, and honestly, I'm no closer to an answer for that question now than I was when I wept while reading Libby's heart-wrenching email. I guess we'll never know this side of heaven.

It took several weeks of wrestling before I was in a position to hear God's voice. Each week I crunched numbers in my little office and thought about MedSend's mission. I thought about how God brought me there. I thought about the bivocational work I was doing as a pastor. I thought about my own journey from being in control of my life's trajectory and defining success—writing my own story—and how that led to surrender.

It was in this broken place that I heard God give me insight on a new mission. How he was going to write the next chapter of my story.

I heard three things:

I am changing the ground rules. Move faster. Think bigger.

Tom and Libby Little made a difference in the world, and they made a difference in my life. I know now what I was only beginning to glimpse then: that God was asking me to continue to surrender and trust Him.

I'm not a doctor. I'm not a missionary. I don't even like hospitals. But somehow, in God's providence and plan, He's asked me to serve Him at MedSend, a medical missions organization.

And it's been the biggest blessing of my life.

I've gone from not trusting God to trusting Him with everything. That has made all the difference in my personal calling and mission.

And the best part? My work with MedSend is simply a single small cog in the wheel of all that God is doing in the world.

WHAT IT MEANS TO LOVE
WITH COMPASSION

This is the beautiful part of how God works. He has equipped us with gifts and abilities to share His message with the world. To love with compassion. To be the conduit through which God can bless.

In the first chapter, we talked about how the world is broken. It's not uncommon to feel like it's getting worse every day and we're powerless to stop it. But what if it didn't have to be that way? What if *you* could do something about it?

What if you decided to . . .

- **Open your heart to compassion**. Hear me out. I'm not saying you aren't compassionate already. But if you're like me, there's more compassion to give. What if we challenged ourselves each day to truly see people the way Jesus does? To overlook their differing ideologies and the things they do that annoy you? To see their souls that are hurting, anxious, and uneasy? What if we opened up our hearts and let down our walls and offered compassion?

- **Love more deeply.** A broken world is filled with broken people. Hurt people. And sometimes hurt people are difficult to love. I know because in the midst of my brokenness, I know I've been difficult to love. But when you see through the eyes of compassion, you can love more deeply. You can recognize the pain that is universal to all of us. Best of all, you can do something about it.

- **Let God work through you.** If there's a connection between the stories in this book and you, it's this: we are only vessels through which God can work. But what a mighty work He can do through one who is surrendered to Him! When you let go and tap into His direction and power, amazing things begin to happen. And when they do, things begin to change.

- **Change the world.** Here's the funny thing about change. We want it to happen quickly, but the most impactful change takes time. You've probably heard the statement that we overestimate what we can do in a year and underestimate what we can do in five years. Every person reading this book can change the world. It's just a matter of willingness to be obedient to your mission and stay the course. Or as Eugene Peterson called it, "a long obedience in the same direction."

Does this excite you like it does me? I hope so, but there's a critical question that we've got to address first:

How do you discover your calling and make it your mission?

Most people either limp through life, with no clear sense of what they are called to do, or they attempt to take control (like I did) and miss what it means to surrender. You can't live out your mission until you discover what it is—which you'll learn how to do in the next section—*and* commit to doing something with what you've learned. Put those two things together, and you can change the world.

THE CALLING QUESTIONS

In Christian circles, has there ever been a more loaded word than the word *calling*?

It sounds so . . . official. Like God chiseled your *one* calling in stone and you have to spend your life digging for the tablets that will give you your life's course and set you free. Like a sort of heavenly scavenger hunt.

That's not how it is at all. We're all called in some way or another. We all have a mission to fulfill. And we all have seasons of life where things change and we move on to different missions. Fortunately, your calling isn't chiseled in stone somewhere. You don't have to spend years searching for it. You don't even have to commit for life. You simply need to walk through a series of questions and do some deep thinking. I'd recommend getting a journal and taking some time to really work through your answers.

Before we start this journey of discovery, I want to encourage you to pray. To open your heart, mind, and soul to God the Father. The Father who loves you, knows you, and seeks to bless you and the world. Consider writing down your prayer so you can refer back to it. The complex mind that God has blessed us with has a downside: we can justify *our* desires and *our* plans and convince ourselves they are from God. The only way I know to push back against this tendency is to pray and listen for God's direction.

Ask for wisdom, discernment, and the power of the Holy Spirit to guide and direct your path. Move slowly, lifting each decision, small and large, to God, with the intent to not get ahead of Him. Test every decision. God will not advise you in opposition to His Word, the Bible. He will not instruct you to do evil or harm yourself or others who love and depend on you. Walk slowly on this journey, listening for the quiet, gentle voice.

Let's dive in.

Question 1: What breaks your heart?

The world is broken—there's no question about that. And a broken world leads to broken hearts. Yours is not immune. But while this can be painful, it can also bring opportunity to right a wrong or fix a problem. This is one of the first questions you need to work through. So dive deep here. What injustice can you not tolerate? What issue brings you to anger or grief? What things are wrong in the world that you would like to see made right?

As a father of four daughters, I simply cannot tolerate the injustice of sex trafficking. I hate it. It truly breaks my heart. That's one of the reasons Katherine Welch's story is so compelling to me. For you it might be something else. God created each one of us with different sensitivities and passions. How you are wired to respond to injustice when you see it is a clue to your calling.

> *Application: Journal your thoughts and see what themes come to the surface. Begin looking for opportunities—this week—to find out how and where you can help.*

Question 2: What are you willing to do about it?

It's one thing to identify what's wrong in the world. It's another to do something about it. Remember, Christians are people of action. So I'd like to challenge you to refuse to look the other way. One of the biggest dangers we face is becoming so busy with life, even the important things of life, that we miss out on our mission. It gets pushed to the back burner as a "someday, maybe" thing. If you've ever read *The Screwtape Letters* by C. S. Lewis, you know that is part of the message of the book: keep people busy so they lose focus on their mission.

To know what breaks your heart is only one half of the equation. That knowledge must be paired with action, and that action must be enhanced by commitment. When I was heartbroken and discouraged after the death of Tom Little, and I felt God telling me to think bigger and move faster, because He was changing the ground rules, I had a choice. I could commit to doing what He said, or I could keep my head down in my little closet crunching numbers and staying busy. I chose the first option, and it has led to a transformation of the ministry of MedSend. But what really excites me is that the best is yet to come.

> *Application: Write a declaration of intent about what you are willing to do to fulfill your mission. Post it somewhere where you can see it every morning.*

Question 3: How has God gifted you to be able to make this your mission?

God is not in the business of calling you to something without equipping you to do that something. The problem is threefold. First, many people never take the time to discover their gifts. Like unopened packages under the Christmas tree, they sit there collecting dust. Every unopened or undiscovered gift is a mission unfulfilled. Second, a lot of people don't recognize that they *are* gifts. Your gift probably comes naturally to you. You may not even realize you are deploying it. Worse yet, you may look at other "gifted" people (often with abilities you don't possess) and compare yourself to them without even realizing they are doing the same thing with you! Your gift is like a fingerprint. It's a unique part of you, and it's waiting to be unleashed. Finally, too many people get in that busy mode I mentioned above, and they are doing everything *but* using their gift. And like a muscle that isn't used, that gift atrophies until it's practically useless.

So don't rush past this too quickly. What are you good at? What brings you joy? Where have you been able to most help others? God just may surprise you by equipping you to do something about the thing that breaks your heart by using the thing that brings you joy. How can you eliminate resistance when following God's call? One way is to understand yourself. How has God uniquely gifted you to make a difference in the world? Your personality, your experiences, your skills. Surrender them all and see what God will do.

Application: Use tools like a spiritual-gifts assessment and StrengthsFinder (there are many more) to dive into your gifts and strengths. Then own them and put them to work.

Question 4: Where can you expand your impact?

This is where the good stuff happens, because although your mission is unique to you, the thing that breaks your heart is breaking others' hearts too. When you align your passion to serve, unlock your gifts and abilities, and partner with others who want to do the same, *that's* when you can really expand your impact. It's the multiplier effect.

It's why MedSend exists.

Think about it for a minute. If we weren't able to relieve the financial burden for the people you read about in this book, what would their stories have looked like instead? Would they have come home sooner? Would they have never gone? Would they have had the mental energy to push through challenges and do the work of ministry God called them to do? Probably not.

I don't write this to brag. I write it to illustrate that when people step into their areas of gifting—MedSend donors who bring the resources, medical professionals who do the hard work of training, mission-minded individuals who follow the call, and even you who read these stories and offer up prayers of support— that is the power of impact. That is unity in the body. That is when kingdom expansion happens, we release the compassion of God to a broken world, and people come face-to-face with Jesus.

WILL YOU?

Which brings us back to you.

The question now is, what are you going to do once you understand *your* mission?

Will you take the first step and follow in obedience? Will you open the door and go talk to your neighbor? Will you reach out to your community? Will you serve in your church? Will you volunteer once a week? Will you start a nonprofit? Will you pack your bags? Will you be the hands and feet of Christ each day, every day?

Will you *love bigger*? Will you look for similarities instead of differences? Will you push past divisions and build unity? Will you see people the way Jesus does and love them anyway? Will you work on yourself to be a person more willing to receive love? Will you let what breaks your heart fill it with love so you are compelled to act?

Will you *serve better*? Will you unleash the power of your gifts and let God work through you? Will you put the needs of others before your own? Will you get uncomfortable? Will you swallow your pride? Will you listen more than you talk? Will you mourn when the going gets tough? Will you be willing to become less than so that He might become more?

Will you *change the world*? Will you open up your mind to the possibility of making true, radical change? Will you do your one small part, over and over again, for as long as it takes? Will you stay the course when you feel discouraged? Will you allow God to be your source and strength? Will you imagine a world that doesn't feel fractured and broken? Will you commit to doing for one what you wish you could do for all?

The need is great. The hearts of people are open. The mission is clear. All it takes is you.

It's time to go.

ACKNOWLEDGMENTS

I want to thank the team at StoryBuilders for their inspiration and dedication in pulling these stories together.

Pastor Jay Button, *For living a life of Christ-like integrity, commitment to others, and perseverance.*

Pastor Steve Treash, *For having the confidence to give me opportunity I did not deserve.*

Pastor Dan McCandless, *For his Christ-like character exhibited to all those he encounters.*

Dr. David Thompson and Dr. Bruce Steffes, *For vision, hard work, and dedication to transform the status quo.*

Dr. Charlie Kelly, *For leading MedSend through turbulent times as Board Chairperson.*

Dr. David Topazian and Drs. Tom and Cynthia Hail, *For without their tireless commitment and dedication, MedSend would not exist.*

I am grateful to have had the opportunity to serve the individuals who participated in this book as well as all those who toil in anonymity providing compassionate healthcare in low-resource areas throughout the world. They are my heroes.

ABOUT THE AUTHOR

Rick Allen is a leading expert on global healthcare delivery in low-resource environments. He is CEO of MedSend, a medical missions organization that has supported over 700 healthcare professionals in 103 countries around the world.

He is the creator of *The Longevity Project*, an innovative MedSend program to protect and support the professional, relational, and spiritual health of healthcare professionals serving in extreme conditions.

As chairman and co-founder of the Institute of Global Healthcare Missions (IGHM), he is focused on scaling physician and nurse training programs throughout Africa and Asia to build local capacity in mission hospitals.

He convenes an annual gathering of organizations focused on faith-based delivery of global healthcare, and he sits on the advisory board of a large faith-based hospital on the Arabian Peninsula.

Prior to his leadership at MedSend, he spent twenty-five years in the software and services industry and eight years as a pastor of a non-denominational church.

For more information about Rick and MedSend, visit medsend.org.

Printed in the USA
CPSIA information can be obtained
at www.ICGtesting.com
CBHW061548090624
9751CB00002B/3